To

Love,

One Street Off Main

Finding my identity

on a road less travelled

Richard Geppinger

This book is dedicated to everyone who has within them
a mind, heart, and spirit that won't settle for the ordinary.

Special thanks go to my mother, grandmother, and sister
for creating a home environment that was loving, fun and safe.

To my wife, Laura, who has given me the priceless world of freedom
and time in which to create and express my gifts, all my love.

To all my friends who never once questioned my tendency to walk
a different path in life, but always reinforced who I was and am.

Most of all,
thanksgiving beyond words goes to the Christ
who rescued me and gave me hope and Life.

Contents

Introduction

Does God really exist? If He does and we are offered eternal happiness, what is there in us that would reject such an offer? You might say, "Sin, of course. Just make a bumper sticker, be done with it and go get a pizza!" Sin, of course is at the root, but it takes more careful thought to understand why we find this same destructive pattern of resistance throughout our lives; to understand and then uproot it. C. S. Lewis put it like this: "We are half-hearted creatures, fooling about with drink and sex and ambition when infinite joy is offered us, like an ignorant child who wants to go on making mud pies in a slum because he cannot imagine what is meant by the offer of a holiday at the sea. We are far too easily pleased" (Lewis, *Glory*, 262). It's easy to settle in here and think this is all there is. Or, that even if Heaven is real, it won't be much fun or we'll be playing harps on clouds like in so many Three Stooges shorts. Rest easy, neither of those scenarios is true. Heaven will exceed any and all of our expectations. God has given us just enough information to encourage us without taking our attention away from Him. Be assured though, many an innocent pizza will come to a pleasant end while writing this book.

For those who know me, I want to take you through my early life and reveal the honest thought processes of a confused and moderately rebellious young man and reveal how I found my true identity out of a very dark and lonely period. For everyone else, I hope that it can be an encouragement as you journey through your own inner struggles about life, faith, and finding meaning in who you really are.

Chapter 1

Receptive

When I was four years old, there was a day I can still remember vividly. It was a summer morning, not yet hot enough to scald my perpetually bare feet. The sun was out in a clear blue sky, but there was nothing otherwise remarkable about it. Yet there I stood in my front yard looking around, and for some reason my brain decided to record it for posterity — and to trouble me later. Why did I make such a lasting impression about nothing in particular? I believe the reason is that it wasn't "nothing." At that age, everything is something and every experience is new. Just being alive was reason enough to celebrate, and if it suddenly came to my mind to strip off my shorts and run around the neighborhood with naught but a smile — then so be it! I am told that happened on more than one occasion. One minute, my mother would look out and see me (with shorts) in our wading pool; the next, there was nothing in the pool except my shorts, slowly drifting around like abandoned tubes on Lazy River at Water World. Teleportation? Hardly. I was running free and creating scenes that were being recorded to trouble other minds later. I'm just glad it was 1964 and not 1969, when I might have inspired adults to do the same.

Record Enabled

My wife Laura gets mad every time I recount something from my childhood. She's accused me of remembering everything short of my trip through the birth canal. The problem now is I can't remember someone's name I just met, and as I watch them walk away, I mentally tag them as another "John Doe." I do have many early memories, but that's nothing to my credit. The only real value they provide is to remind me how alive I felt then and by contrast how dull my edges have since become. That's normal in everyone's life, but the danger comes from forgetting that you ever felt otherwise. In the same way we might look at a mountain scene reflected on the surface of a lake, our childlike wonder serves as a dimmer reflection of what Heaven will be like, and we have mostly forgotten how to experience life like that. Since Laura says she can't recall anything before age nine, it's really quite convenient for her father as he can now tell her they went to all kinds of wonderful and exotic places, and she has to trust him! Those who believe in Christ are told they're about to go to the ultimate Wonderful and Exotic Place, and we must trust Him.

After living in my hometown of Waco, Texas for twenty-six years, I moved to Maine to attend the Shelter Institute, a program teaching self-sufficiency in designing and building your own home. I once again experienced the same sensation that I had felt as a child. All my senses were in "record mode" because I was outside of my familiar surroundings. I think it would be true even if I had moved to an ugly place, but Maine in October is absolutely breathtaking. It looks like God got a little careless and started throwing scarlet paint around, like my sister and I did with Christmas tree icicles. You were supposed to hang each one carefully on only one branch — and don't even *think* about them resting on the one below! After twenty minutes, we thought "Nuts to that!" and began throwing tinsel strands on by the handful. My time in Maine, though short, was the beginning of a great period of re-awakening and growth, and served as a very clear reminder that the adventure doesn't need to end with adulthood.

W.A.C.O.

Let's get something out of the way right now. Waco is not a bad place, and if you started smiling and thinking of crude acronyms because of the association with Branch Davidians, let me remind you that the standoff didn't even happen there, but fifteen miles away in Mount Carmel. It was just easier for CNN to link it with a larger city nearby. That being said, I certainly wouldn't name Waco as the most progressive place to grow up. If truth be told, I'm not even sure they ever experienced the late '60s revolution, but chose instead to drive past that particular exit on the highway of life. That's part of my point in mentioning it, though. My sister Lee Ann and I still had a wonderful childhood there, and were oblivious to the fact that milk curdled on the way home from the market because of the 105-degree heat and humidity of the same percentage. Children are incredibly adaptive and resilient to whatever their environment throws at them. As long as we had some money for ice cream and our baseball didn't sail into a neighbor's forbidden backyard (no one would dare jump the fence because you *knew* their dog was in the bush waiting), we were content. How many adults can say they're content today?

Take a few moments right now and close your eyes. Travel back to your childhood and think about what made you happy. What stands out in the way of simple pleasures?

I'm thinking about some of my own best memories from childhood. Catching lightning bugs, waiting for the ice cream truck to drive through our neighborhood (I can still remember the song it played), the smell of freshly cut grass, and the almost painful anticipation of Christmas morning. We should have that same anticipation of Heaven, not that we should try to set the clock ahead and reach it any sooner! We all have a purpose here and should leave the timing with the One who gave us life in the first place, but when we have the hope of Heaven, we can endure many trials in this life knowing something far better awaits us at the end.

When we are told in the Bible that we need to have the faith of a child, it means a simple faith, not a simple mind. I don't need to set aside my intelligence, just recognize its limitations. God wants us to retain those pure elements we had as children: imagination, laughter, trust, a joyful and unburdened heart, and a belief that anything's possible. Unfortunately, life immediately begins wearing us down through disappointment, pain (both physical and emotional) and the injustices we see. In the same way that we use our leg muscles to resist gravity's unrelenting downward pull, we try to uphold our youthful enthusiasm and belief that the world's a good place; but without the additional input of divine truth and hope, our emotions, just like our leg muscles, become tired and we become exhausted and cynical. This also explains why one negative comment stays with us throughout the day instead of the ten positive ones: we're already fighting gravity as we climb the ladder ("Say, brother, mind if I hang another ten-pound weight from your ankle?"). It's easy to begin doubting God's goodness or involvement if we only look at the stormy sea around us. Of course, most of what we see in the world as far as pain goes is actually what we do to ourselves and others, but it's far easier to blame God than to take responsibility.

All these things can affect our view and confidence in God if we don't think them through. In the end, I can't ask Him why He allowed something to happen. The terrifying consequences of Free Choice are self-evident. If I eat a chicken-fried steak and have clogged arteries later, I can't blame Him, except for making it delicious. God doesn't have an "Undo" button. My only real question now is why He didn't throw Satan into the pit when he rebelled, instead allowing him to take so much of humanity with him. To that, I have no answer. I'll have to wait to ask that and other questions ("Can you tell me again about the grand purpose behind chiggers?") when I see Him face to face. I have a feeling that when I do see God, I really won't care any longer.

Disappointment

I can't help but feel that as we grow older, a large part of our cynicism comes from a false expectation of who we believe God is and what we think His promises to us are. I grew up watching my mother struggle with the knowledge that God is all powerful and yet He allows His children to suffer. How do you bridge that apparent gap? As we watched her waste away from cancer in 1984, we prayed for her to be healed based on scriptures that we had always held on to "... and the prayer offered in faith will restore the one who is sick" (James 5:15 NASB). Did He fail us, or did we misunderstand and try to claim something that obviously isn't always true?

When my mother died, we borrowed our church van and carried her body back to Kenton, Oklahoma, and buried her in the wild and beautiful cemetery overlooking the Cimarron river. I had brought my acoustic guitar and I was sitting outside alone that evening playing when I suddenly felt her presence around me. I didn't see a vision of her or anything like that, but I knew beyond anything I know now that all was well with her, and there was no longer any veil between her and her Creator. Whatever the full explanation is behind that event, it was a gift to me, and His peace that enveloped me that evening is unlike anything else I've ever experienced. It wasn't transcendental or otherworldly, but like the most comforting and familiar experiences we have here on earth all rolled together, then magnified by 100. A mild midsummer evening with friends, a warm bath, a sweet but subtle scent. It was as if my very core was smiling. It was absolutely a calm that no storm could disturb. You can't feel that Presence and not trust, even when He takes someone you love.

God isn't like a dimmer switch, somewhere between on and off. He is either 100 percent good or not. So, if He is good (which I believe) then everything He allows is good for us in some way, even if we can't understand it now. If you're familiar with the story about Joseph in the Old Testament, you know that his brothers sold him into slavery. After God elevated him to a position of authority under Pharaoh, his brothers came seeking food in a time of severe famine. After he told them who he was, they were understandably worried!

Joseph's response to them was amazing: "Do not be afraid, you meant evil against me, but God meant it for good..." (Gen. 37-50 NASB). It's an incredible account of God's sovereign control, and it goes back to having the faith of a child. There's complete rest there.

Chapter 2

Of Grice and Men

That same year I was standing in my yard on Grice Drive looking up at the blue sky in happy innocence, my father divorced my mother. For all my very early memories from age four and under, I don't have that many of us as a complete family unit. My dad was Air Force and so we dutifully moved around to several places, yet there are a few memories that stand out in my mind during our short tenure in Omaha, Nebraska, when I would have been three.

We had a sliding back door with wind chimes singing nearby and I had the brilliant idea of how to save the wonderful snow that had just fallen. Mr. Sun was out and doing significant damage to this white miracle, so I started bringing the snow in and hiding it behind our couch to protect it from melting. My plan of salvation was soon discovered by He-Who-Must-Not-Be-Disobeyed. I must have blacked out or something because I can't remember anything after that...

Another one was us at the dinner table. I had been unfairly portioned a head-sized dollop of boiled spinach and was attempting to wash each bite down with my milk. My childish calculations were off and I ran out of milk with half-ahead of green moss left. I kindly asked for more milk and was refused until I finished my task at hand. Father and son each stood their ground until size finally decided matters. I would be sequestered in Lee Ann's and my shared bedroom until I finished my spinach. I was mortified and deeply troubled, until I noticed my sister's doll. My, what a big mouth she had!

Dolly was stuffed (literally) and saved from certain starvation and I was released from temporary exile and brought back into the Promised Land, which flowed with milk and honey buns. I don't recall that particular discovery and resulting consequence at all. Must have been another blackout.

Introduction to Marketing

Several years later, some genius at a marketing firm decided to label their client's spinach can with the image of Popeye. Well, of course it would taste better, right? Every kid in America must have cried out for mom to go and get some spinach (with very explicit directions about the label). Those moms must have wondered what in the world got into their kid, but being wise they immediately went to Piggly Wiggly grocery store and got some. After all, you never look a gift Wiggly in the mouth (good advice, regardless). A friend's mother bought several cans and invited me over. We forced all we could down our gullets and then ran for the mirror, expecting to witness grotesquely massive forearms. What we saw instead was puny and in desperate need of Charles Atlas. Disillusionment with the adult world now entered our trusting little minds, later reinforced by Atlas' disappointing muscle program and pretty much everything else you found on the back of comic books. X-Ray Specs? Just a feather in each lens to diffuse your vision and create the illusion of seeing through solid objects, which probably resulted in kids getting glasses much earlier in life.

An interesting side note: another good friend and I finally ordered Sea Monkeys in our late teens just to satisfy our curiosity about these mysterious little beasties, all the while still secretly hoping they would actually wear crowns and sport tridents like they pictured. We treated the water with the included solution, and then had to wait overnight (grrr!). The next morning dawned and tearing open the packet of life, we emptied the powder into the water. We watched closely as each particle sank toward the bottom and noticed that some of them began to wiggle and swim around. What in the world were these things? The following day, they were big enough to see each one a little more clearly, and we saw to our disappointment that neither spear nor crown was present, though there was one that appeared to have enormous genitalia or some other anatomical complication. He swam more slowly than the others and provided mild entertainment for the rest of the day. We found out they were (SPOILER ALERT) brine shrimp. I'm guessing that they eventually enjoyed a thrilling ride down my friend's toilet.

The last memory I have of our house in Omaha consists of my sister somehow talking me into climbing in our metal trash can and allowing her to push me down a hill on our property. All other things being equal — I puked. That may be the sole reason why I still can't abide carnival rides that spin. Didn't think about that until just now.

What Goes Around

I was born at Connally Air Force Base in Waco; then we moved to Roswell, Amarillo, Omaha, and then finally back to Waco when I was four. I remember us pulling into our driveway at 752 Grice Drive late one night and immediately looking toward my friend Clay Marshall's house down the street. I'm troubled at this memory because it would mean that I knew and remembered him at the age of one or less. Rather than risk being bopped in the back of my head by my wife, I think I'll go with "misplaced memory" and leave it at that. It must have been another late arrival that I'm picturing instead. I wish memories had time stamps like our digital photos do because I have lots of snapshots from a very early age that I can't place.

Our street and neighborhood was a wonderful place to grow up. There were lots of kids our age and we could all walk to school together. The municipally owned Lion's Park was relatively close by and we almost lived there. Mom bought us summer passes and we walked there almost every day, playing mini-golf, swimming, and riding their small assortment of carnival rides (that didn't spin). It was only a mile or so from our house, but to our short legs striding through the sweltering Texas heat, it seemed like forever! We would often say to each other, "Aren't you glad we're not just starting?!" We might only have reached the end of our street at that point, but it still made us feel better just to say it.

Our home was part of a semicircle, and Grice Dr. was connected at both ends to another street named Greer (like the letter "D," so there wasn't much traffic) and that allowed us kids to basically commandeer the place. We played baseball and kickball; we flew kites and ran from the bats. It was great! It also allowed the older kids (our parents) to have block parties where they could literally block off both ends and fire up the grills all around. That was the first time someone introduced us to Mr. Pibb and it felt like such a betrayal. Dr Pepper was Waco's own invention starting in 1885, and we were loyal subjects to that pure cane sugar in liquid form. We also courted Big Red in a Big Way, but our hearts truly belonged to the "good Dr."

There was also a network of tunnels nearby, and many of us explored those as far as we dared, often carrying matches or candles to see by. It's a good thing Stephen King hadn't written *It* yet! One day, Clay and I were playing down there and he tried getting into a particularly small feeder and got stuck trying to turn around. We both panicked (which made him swell up like a toad) and we wondered how we would ever get him free without bringing in the "Paddling Cavalry." We finally got him free on our own and I'll never forget the sight of him jumping up and down in his newfound freedom. The next day, we had one of those "gully-washer" rainstorms and we looked in horror at that same tunnel opening as we drove by; it was completely filled with rushing water emptying into the creek.

For many years, I would have a recurring dream in which Clay and I traveled deep into those tunnels, choosing left and right branches in a labyrinthine nightmare, far beyond recovery or hope of ever finding our way back. Then we would see a faint light ahead, and with the tunnel getting smaller and smaller (claustrophobic yet?), I would come to a little hole that

I could look up through and see into my own kitchen. I was looking though our sink drain and everything I loved was right there! If only I could somehow get past the strainer, I would be home and spared the endless journey back through the tunnels — then I would wake up. I realize there's enough psychological material in that dream for an entire conference, but I won't go there.

The End of an Era

My sister, who had the privilege of being born in the exotic land of Landstuhl, Germany, is nearly four years older than I am and because she was eight at the time, our father's abandonment affected her deeply; much more deeply than I was. I didn't feel his absence until later, when we should have been playing baseball, camping and fishing like other fathers and sons. I only remember my mother talking to him once in a while on the phone and usually weeping at the end. THAT was my sole distress at the time — her pain.

Dad came to visit us once or twice, and we traveled to his home in Seattle on two separate occasions, but other than talking on the phone once in a while, there really wasn't much contact and I didn't miss his presence at the time. Our first visit there included our mother and we all stayed on his boat in Puget Sound. We had a lot of fun traveling through the Hiram M. Chittenden Locks, swimming in the ocean and fishing, where I caught my first and only shark. I wasn't aware of much tension between my mom and him at that time. The second visit was even more fun. Lee Ann and I flew alone this time and Robert Geppinger had remarried by then. His new wife, Sylvia, had two children our age from her previous marriage and we all got along wonderfully. I've often wondered what life would have been like if Dad had remained with us. There certainly would have been a military-type discipline and I wouldn't have been able to grow my hair long, which I did when I turned eleven. I'm sure I would have benefited in several unknown ways, but I can't help but be thankful for our family as it was, and was just about to become.

Chapter 3

Grace in Times of...

We were living in Amarillo, Texas when my father left and my maternal grandparents, Richard and Grace, decided to move back to Waco with us. My grandfather had cancer and died within a year. Now there was deep trauma for both Grace and her newly divorced daughter and so it was decided that my grandmother should stay and live with us permanently. It made perfect sense as it was mutually beneficial for everyone. Grace had a home and family and my mother had help raising two young children. It sure didn't hurt that Grace was a former school teacher either! Her knowledge and wisdom would be called upon many times in the future. And so our little broken family of four moved along and adjusted to this new incarnation. Lee Ann and I were truly blessed with having people in our daily lives that not only deeply loved us, but sincerely modeled their faith in God in a practical way that would provide an unparalleled foundation for us to stand on. To this day, I can't think of anyone who is a better example of what it means to be Christian than my mother and grandmother. They were both exceptionally good with people. My grandmother was born with deformed feet and though she used crutches when going out (and sometimes at home), most of the time she scooted around our hardwood floors on her knees using small pillows. That was how we knew her and it seemed perfectly normal to us. I can still remember the distinctive sound of her moving around our house in Waco. There simply can't be anyone else on earth who had more natural patience than Grace did. She had a brilliant mind and was always busy with some project, like translating books into French or Spanish, writing poetry, designing her dream house (can't wait to see what she has in Heaven now!), or tracing our ancestry. Apparently, we had a distant relative who once resided in the famous Neuschwanstein Castle in Bavaria. I don't know his station in life — he may have been only a boot cleaner — but still, one takes what one can get.

Amazing Grace

Even in the exacting memory of childhood, I can't recall one single instance when I came into my grandmother's bedroom, interrupting her work with some childhood speculation, that she didn't show honest delight to see me. There was never even a hint that I was a bothersome nuisance. It was not coincidence that she was named Grace. Later, many people would call her Amazing Grace. I remember sitting together, looking at a mirror and wondering whether my eyesight or the reflection was bouncing. We had many, many fun and interesting discussions together like that. She loved science, too, and we always got along effortlessly. I say that, but I have another thought clamoring for mention: she loved to clean and often had company from around the country stop by to visit, usually with only a phone call to mention they were in town and on their way over. That's when her "scooting sound" was feared by Lee Ann and me. We suddenly had twenty minutes to get things straightened up and presentable!

Another fearsome task, worthy of the slaves of Pharaoh, was a solid brass table about four feet in diameter that my mother brought back from Morocco. It had details up the ying yang and it was our duty to polish it with some sort of hideous paste. Rubbing like our lives depended on reaching the genie inside, we would scrub until it left us exhausted. The yings were easy, but the yangs were something else. Gads! The other annual torment my sister and I endured was painting our kitchen cabinets. They had so many coats of white paint on them, they must have been twice their original thickness by the time we sold the house and moved away. What haunts me in my dreams even now is the astounding question of why we didn't use semigloss enamel, so we could just wipe all the hand prints off! Instead, we always used flat latex — the kind that absorbs everything and can't be cleaned. We must have had a windfall of the accursed stuff, because I can't think of any other reason why four intelligent human beings and a dog wouldn't have thought of that.

A Slip of the Tongue

We knew Grace's father had been a mean man and that her mother eventually divorced him for fear that Grace's brother might kill him one day in her defense. Divorces were rare in those days, but he was physically abusive and she was smart and practical enough to know the right thing to do and follow though with it. It wasn't until Grace was in her mid- or late eighties that Lee Ann and I heard her say something that dropped both of our jaws. She was talking about something else entirely, but as often happens when you get older, this closely kept detail just came out without her intending it to.

Grace said that her father had once pushed her mother down a flight of stairs while she was pregnant...with her! THAT was why she had been born with deformed feet. We simply couldn't believe our ears. We had lived with Grace almost our entire lives and had never heard this before. Why? Because when she forgave someone, there wasn't any reason to bring it up again.

Even now, I have to catch my breath when I think about it. We all know people (that includes me) who talk about some past injury they sustained and how they forgave the offending person. That is fairly common and even commendable, but this was on a whole different level. From her perspective, when you truly forgive someone, that means you don't need to talk about it. Don't get me wrong, there are times when it's good and cathartic to talk about those things, but it also reveals that there can be a darker motive involved. Lifting yourself up while putting someone else down (look how awful this person was, but I ROSE to the occasion and forgave them!). Do you see the delicate trap that any of us can fall into? Even such a charitable and loving end can have a donkey tail attached to it. Grace's whole life was devastatingly impacted by someone else's cruel action, but she didn't allow it to cause bitterness in her heart or use it as an excuse to not accomplish things in life. Amazing Grace.

That my father would one day fear for his soul (because of his lifestyle) and turn to the mother of the one he had hurt and abandoned years before, tells you the enormous respect he had for Grace. She of course prayed for and comforted him in her sweet spirit and I am convinced that he is in Heaven right now, and that we will see him one day. It's also my suspicion that by fully understanding the hurt he caused our family (and my sister in particular), our Lord will allow him to do something very special in the preparation for our arrival Home. Maybe he's building Lee Ann's eternal dwelling right now.

Her Normal

Grace's relationship to God was almost otherworldly. She had developed a closeness to Him that made it seem almost casual for her. To the rest of us, we were simply in awe. She would mention astounding things as mere details, like Moses might have done as he told his wife a story over dinner: "Honey, I was parting the sea today, when the darndest thing happened...." At some point in her life, she had so embraced His truth and committed to walking with Him daily that it really did became natural for her. There was no religion in our home at all. There was love, devotion, and absolute common sense. What a huge difference that last one makes! Michael Stipe (the lead singer for R.E.M.), sang about losing his religion and I have to say kudos to that. Lose it and find something far better in relationship instead.

Growing up in the tiny ranch community of Kenton, Oklahoma must have been both sweet and burdensome for my grandmother. Burdensome, because everyone knew what everyone else was doing. There was a dance being held one night and my then-teenaged mother longed to go! Grace knew she would be looked down on by the religious of the day for giving her permission — who would see it as akin to performing voodoo and sacrificing bunnies around a bonfire. That didn't stop her, though, because she had common sense. "Of course you can go! Have fun," was her reply.

Because our mother worked full time, it fell to my grandmother to feed us and she did remarkably well at it. Unfortunately, she didn't write down many of her delicious recipes, preferring to memorize them instead. Lee Ann did a great job of recreating a lot of the best ones after our grandmother passed away. Again, it was only late in life that we found out that she didn't like to cook at all. Another mindblower because she did it every day for us and we never would have guessed the truth. It was done, not with pearls around her neck (like June in *Leave It to Beaver*), but with genuine goodwill and cheerfulness. Everything she did was cheerfully performed with a true servant's heart. She later made a covenant with the Lord that involved me.

Chapter 4

Don't Call Me Pat

Patricia Lee Eddy was born February 3, 1930 and it was her small fear that God would one day call her "Pat" in Heaven. I can't say I blame her when I think about the difference in hearing the beautiful and elegant "Welcome, Patricia, to your new Home," rather than "Yo, Pat! How's it hangin'?" There were a few friends who called her Pat, including one little urchin my age. That one particularly galled her.

If my grandmother was a stalwart tower, my mother was the cable car that swung freely from it. She was capable of more emotional highs and lows and was also more outgoing and relational. Maybe my own dichotomy comes from those two influences. I'm both perfectly at ease and happy when I'm alone as well as when I'm surrounded by friends and strangers. Patricia loved people and she was loved by everyone who knew her. Doctors and plumbers alike felt like they could talk to her, because she had that special gift of putting everyone around her at ease, no matter what their background was. My grandmother wasn't that physically affectionate, but my mother was all hugs. We got along very well, except when I grew older and then had to duck under her arms to avoid smooches and being taught how to dance in the kitchen. She worked for Braniff Airlines and really was a beautiful woman. Patricia Lee Eddy should have been picked up by a special man and treasured forever, but that just never happened. There were several professional men in our life who I believe would have, except they were already married.

Mom had a wicked sense of humor and really was the life of the party wherever she went. This wonderful trait, which should have been celebrated, may have been a source of trouble in her marriage to my father. Both my sister and I think he had an insecurity that made him resent her popularity with their friends and the public in general. While they were stationed in Germany, she played a pipe organ at a church cathedral each Sunday and was a very gifted musician. At functions or parties, Patricia might suddenly break out of Bach into some sort of boogie-woogie and everyone would gather around to laugh and sing all the songs that they knew. That seemed to really bother my father. My mother loved holidays and any occasion that allowed a party to happen, and I certainly have lots of memories of get-togethers at our home in Waco.

Rock-and-Roll and Party Every Day

We were very blessed to have Patricia as our mother. We played games together, celebrated the Fourth of July with homemade ice cream and fireworks. Birthdays were wonderful and Christmas morning was full of presents and holiday cheer. She did everything within her power to enable us to grow up knowing we were loved and capable of anything. We were introduced to tennis, bowling, baseball, swimming. Anything we were interested in doing, she would find a way for us to be involved, even with our limited finances.

As I learned to play guitar, she would listen to the music I was interested in and figure out how to play it with me. This meant emulating Keith Emerson from Emerson Lake & Palmer, Rick Wakeman from Yes, or Led Zeppelin's John Paul Jones playing "No Quarter". Pretty amazing when you think about what she grew up listening to. Sometimes I paid for this benefit dearly with a request to accompany her at church as she played accordion.

We sometimes struggled to pay bills and she modeled a proper response by having us all gather together and pray for God to meet our needs, which He always did through various means. One time an anonymous letter arrived with $100 cash in it and we were able to pay the electric bill that month. It drew our little family closer together and cemented the fact that we could always count on God, as well as each other. "We" against the world always feels better than "Me" against anything.

In Contrast

Growing up with a mother who already had one foot in Heaven had to be hard, and I know my mother struggled with trying to measure up to Grace's example. You can't measure up to someone else's example. You can be inspired and learn many things from others, but you are still your own person by design, and you need to make peace with that truth and grow within your own environment. Another battle for Mom was trying to reconcile a God who was all powerful and yet allowed His children to suffer. Welcome to the other several billion people who struggle with that, too.

I can well remember times when her pain and frustration became too much and she would literally yell at God. Of course, she would feel so guilty about doing that and then feel even more inadequate next to my grandmother. Grace would be the first one to console and reassure her that God didn't mind being yelled at. Observing this, even at a young age, I understood that He would rather us yell at Him than just ignore Him. At least we are still communicating on some level, and though He would prefer that we trust Him and experience the peace that comes with that, He understands our heart's cry and uses the channel of communication that is still open and available for Him to speak into our lives. When you think about it, her yelling only exhibited a different kind of faith. She knew Him to be better than her understanding or circumstances suggested and this was expressed with frustration, and sometimes anger. As a nurse, Mom would have preferred that we didn't *ever* hurt ourselves, but thankfully, she didn't try to prevent us from exploring and experimenting our way through several trips to the ER for stitches, either. God also allows us to climb trees and fall. One day, all creation will be remade and pain will be done away with forever — but until then, this is our reality. I never suffered a broken bone until I was forty and fell on my head. Another story.

House Calls

After working at Braniff, Patricia started working at a doctor's office, and that was great since we were always stepping on a nail or getting sick. It's hard to believe that doctors made house calls back then, but they did, and our Dr.

William Avent probably went above and beyond even that common practice because she worked for him. He was very kind, but also intimidating as he would lean back against a counter or wall, crossing both his arms and ankles as he decided what to do with me. This usually meant a shot of some kind, gamma globulin being the worst and most painful because it was like injecting cold molasses very slowly. I remember hearing the executioner's call one time and then running around the office table as they chased me. I have no problem with needles or getting an IV now, but it was a different story back then, as it is for most children. In spite of the fact that he often administered the pain, I still had a lot of respect for Dr. Avent.

It was therefore a boy's dream that three decades later, in 1997, I would make a trip back home to Waco and end up staying with him in his home for a week. I had received news that a dear childhood friend of mine had died. I missed being there with my friend, Steve Morales, by only two weeks. That made me plan a trip back home to Waco after being gone for ten years. I was determined to find every close personal friend, and friend of our family, to let them all know what they meant to me. I arrived without a place to stay and a coworker of my mom immediately called Dr. Avent to let him know I was in town. He invited me to come and stay. His wife was in long-term care and I think it was a comfort for him to have someone else there in his now too-quiet home. We stayed up late, sitting on his bed in our pajamas, laughing and watching ball games, or walking around his beautiful neighborhood talking about astronomy. I couldn't get over this amazing feeling of talking with someone who had always been so much older and out of intellectual reach; yet there we were as adults, communicating on a whole different level. It gave me a preview of what Heaven will be like when there won't be any age difference between anyone. Can you imagine hanging out with your parents and grandparents (not to mention people who lived thousands of years ago) just like you do with your best friends now?

A couple of years later, I was talking on the phone with that same coworker and she told me Dr. Avent had passed away. I was feeling so thankful that he and I had that opportunity to experience something so rare and how much it had meant to me personally. She then told me that he never stopped talking about "that time Richard came to stay with me." That amazing thought still warms my heart.

Stand-Alone Goodness

There was nothing but kindness and earthly goodness in my mother, and people picked up on that immediately. If I broke up with a girlfriend, there would usually be no more contact between us, but she would often continue to write my mother for months or even years afterward. She had that kind of impact on everyone. Even though we had a wonderfully close relationship and great communication, I still look forward to one day telling her how thankful I am for everything she did for me in providing a completely safe and loving environment.

A perfect example of how comforting and full of common sense she was came in about as awkward a situation that you could imagine as a young boy. My friends and I had discovered some *Playboy* and *Penthouse* magazines that had been thrown away and I had taken one into our bathroom to peruse (probably just looking for articles on kite making or something...). A few minutes after returning to my room, there was a knock on my door. My mother came in and sat down on my bed beside me, said "You forgot something," and handed me my magazine. I had left it sitting wide open in the bathroom! I felt like I was turning inside out in my embarrassment and humiliation. I had absolutely nothing to say. She, however, spoke right up and told me how normal my curiosity was and that I could always feel free to ask her anything I wanted to know about sex and females. I probably muttered my thanks and then she left my room. What an incredibly wise way to handle that awkward situation! No yelling, no preaching, no ignoring or denial — just sound advice and recognition of an opportunity to engage in honest, healthy conversation with her young son. She had no precedent in her youth with this same topic from her mother, but she still knew the right way to handle it when the time came. Amazing Patricia.

Chapter 5

A Short Aside

As I'm sitting here beside our Christmas tree writing this book, I'm once again recognizing a pattern that has been with me as far back as I can remember: a tendency to work in a finished format right from the start.

This first became apparent as I started taking art classes when I was twelve years old. All art students know you're supposed to start drawing a person by sketching out oval or round outlines to get the basic shape, and then bring in more detail as you progress. I never worked that way or developed that habit because it seemed like a waste of time to draw something that you were just going to immediately erase. So instead, I would end up with a head that was shaded and complete in every detail, but without a body.

In grade school when I played clarinet, I never learned to read music because I would take the music home and memorize it on the instrument instead of reading it from the score. Even today when I'm playing at church on the worship team, I memorize all the music so I can engage with the congregation instead of looking down at sheet music.

When I recorded "Laura's Song" as a surprise for my wife's birthday, I had sixteen tracks of instrumentation done — complete with levels and effects — that only amounted to twenty-three-seconds, but with no idea where I was going from there! I can see how it would be more efficient to lay everything out first, but I just don't work that way. I create from inspiration, and I work best when I immerse myself in the finished sight or sound environment. It's kind of cyclic, if you think about it; being inspired by your own inspiration. Kind of like unrolling the carpet you're actually walking on.

This was especially true as I recorded my *Early Reflections* DVD in 5.1 surround. You never print an effect to tape because you commit yourself, and then it's almost impossible to go back and correct anything or change the level of that effect. However, the influence and inspiration that came from hearing all those early sound reflections had such a major impact on what I was composing and how I was performing, I needed to experience it in real time while I wrote and recorded each song. A certain chord or combination of notes might not sound very good dry, but it became magical when immersed in that particular reverb. The same was true in reverse; something might sound wonderful dry, but sound too blurred in this cathedral-like space. It really affected what I wrote and how I performed.

And so it is even now. I started writing this book within iBooks Author because I like to see the finished product and how it will look and flow as an e-book. I had to stop and switch to Scrivener, however, because it's too hard to export the text for other proprietary formats from within the Author app.

There may be psychological elements that you can read into all this — and some of them may be legitimate. I will just chalk it up as more evidence that I'm one street off Main.

C'est la vie.

Chapter 6

8 to ∞

Anytime Billy Graham came on TV, we would all sit and watch it together as a family. To this day, I have a soft spot for "Just as I Am" because of those televised crusades. It should be noted that three decades later, I would get to meet George Beverly Shea and get his autograph. It's funny how a Zeppelin-loving guitarist would be so thrilled to meet someone so far on the "uncool" side of the musical spectrum. I was high up in the stands at a Christian Artists concert at the YMCA in Estes Park when I spotted him and quickly swung down like a monkey to tell him how much he meant to our family. I don't think he was as thrilled to meet me. There's a *Simpsons* episode ("Bart on the Road") where the schoolyard terror, Nelson, makes Bart stop on their underage road trip in order to watch an Andy Williams concert, and looks on with rapturous glee when he sings "Moon River." There must be that same latent potential in all of us when we connect to some childhood memory, or relate to a beloved family member's interest, vicariously enjoyed.

Something in Billy's message one night when I was eight years old deeply stirred my young heart and I began weeping. My mother took me into my room so we could talk and I accepted Jesus as my Savior that night. Many people may have had an experience where they felt pressured or compelled into a decision of faith at too early an age, but I can assure you that was not the case with me. I knew exactly what I was feeling and wanted, and I knew from that moment on that I would go to Heaven when I died and that a personal relationship had begun. What I didn't know at that tender age was that my belief would later be tested to its breaking point.

My mother played piano and organ at Emmanuel Baptist Church in Waco, and of course my sister and I went there as well. It was a fairly large church (but nothing like some of today's megasized behemoths) with a good mixture of Baylor students and older people. There weren't a lot of kids my age, however, so church on Sunday became something like an exception to regular life for me; the right thing to do but not a lot of fun, with no connection to my real life and friends. I remember summers in particular when Vacation Bible School seemed like a rude intrusion, and there were many times when Clay Marshall and I would hide behind his house when we saw the church bus coming down our street to pick everyone up.

I'm not absolutely sure about the timeline, but it may have been around the age of eleven or twelve when I decided I didn't want to go to church anymore. I'm sure my mother was concerned and disappointed but she still let me make my choice. I'm also sure that she and my grandmother spent many nights praying for my safety. It's not easy to let someone you love detach themselves from your proven experience and wisdom and grow on their own, but they were both wise enough to understand that I was beginning to rebel and test the waters in which I found myself swimming. They had to trust that I would be okay in the end.

To Flea or Not to Flea

As a family, we would pray together and read the Bible, but it wasn't in a formal way or on a daily schedule. We all talked about our individual problems very openly and prayed specifically about those concerns. Prayer meetings usually amounted to all of us piling onto Grandmother's bed. There was no music unless our dog, Tricia, decided to join us up there and then there might be some high-pitched wailing coming from Grace. She was of the old-school belief that pets should be mostly outside entities, not sleeping on the bed right across from her, tightly nestled against her beloved daughter, sharing her fleas and other adventures. For fleas Tricia had in abundance, and there didn't seem to be anything we could do about it. We would have her dipped at the vet and then powder her within an inch of her life only to release her into our backyard with a tail of white streaming behind her that would put any comet to shame. From Tricia, they proliferated onto our furniture, and years later I came in to find my bass player sitting on our couch looking frantically at his bare chest, trying to solve the distressing riddle of feeling and seeing black specks appear and disappear on his skin right before his eyes.

As for my grandmother, I have vivid memories of her pecking away on her old Royal typewriter and then suddenly stopping and looking at Tricia, who just lay there looking angelic, and proclaiming, "I think that damn dog is passing wind." And she'd stick out her chin in mock indignation. Proper blame was never ascertained but we all cackled with laughter because their relationship was so comical. The closest she ever got to actually petting her was talking softly and rubbing the air six inches above her head, but Tricia was suitably appreciative and wagged her tail in rapturous delight. One of the most comedic moments between the two came from our grandmother losing her dentures. We looked high and low and prayed about finding them for two days. I think she had just about given up when I heard a strange sound coming from the kitchen. I couldn't tell if someone was laughing or crying, so I ran in there and behold, they had been found...in Tricia's water dish. We were laughing so hard and trying to figure out how to break the news to her. We all thought she would immediately throw them out and buy a new set, but being from that practical generation, she merely rinsed them under the faucet and back in they went!

Foundational Lessons

All these little episodes were teaching and demonstrating to me that prayer is a practical thing. God was supposed to be an everyday part of our lives, not just on Sunday. I'm sure some of this was sinking in, but when all your needs are being met at that age, you really don't think that much about it. I went on with my simple life and tried to believe all I was being taught. Having guardians who truly love you and demonstrate their faith makes all the difference in the world in how you process doctrines about an invisible world. You can't see God but you are told that He is everywhere and looking out for you. Road rash, toothaches and stitches begin to clarify the terms somewhat. Okay, maybe He is looking out for us, but that doesn't mean pain won't find you. Somewhere there is commonality and reconciliation between reality and concept. He protects us from some things but obviously not everything. How does that work? When will He and when won't He?

At fifty-four years of age, I wish I had a clear-cut answer to that fundamental question, but I still don't and no one else does either. I don't think it came to my young mind yet, but what about those who were not spared? We all show our gratitude and thanksgiving for those who narrowly miss being injured or killed, but what about the person next to them who didn't make it? This seems to be especially true in tornado country, where multiple vortices obliterate one home and leave the one next to it untouched. How do you process that in light of an all-loving, all-powerful God? Why was one protected and the other taken? These are very legitimate questions, and yet, as I look at the number 54 again, I'm suddenly struck by how absurdly small it is. Even 88 or 103 is almost immeasurably small compared to eternity, so how, within reason, could I expect to have the whole universe figured out? It's kind of crazy and yet I think all of us have the expectation that we should be able to answer those kinds of questions. What if we simply don't have mental equipment that is adequate for the task? What if it's not only a matter of missing information that prevents us from finding an answer, but having a CPU that can't possibly crunch all the numbers involved? More than that, it may even be a form of mathematical equation that we don't even know exists! But there's something in me — and all of us — that still thinks we should be able to figure it out: the finite knowing and totally understanding the Infinite. And yet in this very real world we live in, all we are often left with is mystery and the need to trust, and that's an injury to our personal and collective pride.

Insight into Large-Scale Disaster

I will share one occasion that happened many years later that troubled me so much I had to ask God to help me process it. I don't know if the answer I received the next day will make sense or comfort you at all, or if it was only meant for me and the way I think, but I will try to explain it and hope it helps you, too. The 2004 tsunami took approximately 228,000 lives. How is it humanly possible to wrap your mind around such an overwhelming disaster? How could God allow this to happen? In response to my prayer, I was given to understand that our exponential horror is directly related to the magnitude and concentration of death at a specific event; that the idea of seeing so many lives lost at the same time is somehow more horrific and outrageous than the single death we saw on the news last night. This is wrong and based on a purely human value. Death itself is the worst thing we can witness. That any person should ever die is unimaginably tragic, but we don't see it that way. Instead, we fall apart emotionally and often become extremely angry at God only when it's large-scale or personal. A sudden inspiration caused me to research how many people died around the world every day. The answer?

150,000

Two-thirds of the same amount of people die *every single day* and that doesn't bother us at all. That's the equivalent of 240 identical tsunamis a year! Why aren't we in continual mourning about this? It's true that most people aren't aware of that fact, but be honest: now that you do know, does it affect you the same way? What if I told you that the equivalent of

9/11 happens more than twice a day here in the United States? That's right, 7,115 die in our own country every day of the year, and yet we go on with our daily lives and don't give it a thought. Death is tragic — period. It doesn't matter how many or in what fashion — death is tragic. The other true and relatively comforting realization was that each person who died in the 2004 tsunami only died once. That may appear to be a ridiculous statement, but it seems to be another aspect of human nature to somehow absorb the total terror we feel from witnessing the enormity of a tragedy, and then project it onto each person's experience as they met their end. The truth is that it probably wasn't any worse than what someone feels when their car slides on ice and they face a head-on collision, or the skydiver who realizes the chute didn't open and sees the unforgiving earth rushing to meet them. There's some momentary terror, to be sure, but not a magnified and collective share of it as we might imagine.

You may ask how I "heard from God" in response to my prayer. There are only a handful of times that I prayed with such serious and earnest attention regarding a puzzling question. Each time, I had previously thought hard about the given situation, seeking a logical answer, but without success. I recognized it to be an answer from Him because it produced peace, first of all, and because it came to me each time instantly as a complete picture, effortlessly and usually when I wasn't even thinking about it. There was no linear process of thought involved. I picture it now as the difference between a 5,400 rpm computer hard drive spinning to access information, and the instant retrieval of a solid state-drive. I don't possess a solid-state drive.

On the Lighter Side

The writers of *The Simpsons* have the uncanny and brilliant ability to capture the absurdity of life and our common humanity in honest and humorous ways. Such as...

~ Springfield Picnic ~
Fine dining in a bee-filled atmosphere
(or)
"God welcomes His victims"

...on the church sign outside. That's so funny because we do run to the same One to be comforted, who we also think brought it on us in the first place, and at whom we are also currently mad. It exposes us in our contradiction.

One of my favorite *Simpson* lines comes from Christian wife, Maude Flanders, after their home (and only theirs) is totally destroyed by a hurricane. Crawling out from under the bathtub, she says to her nauseatingly good husband, "Oh Neddy, it was terrifying. I thought I was headed for the eternal bliss of Paradise!" No matter what we say we believe, we're all afraid of the unknown.

New Heights

That He does in fact hear our prayers and protect us, I have no trouble believing because I really don't think I would be here writing this if my family had not been praying for me. Anyone growing up in the South is very familiar with the alternating red and white radio towers. We had two just up the street, and I can still see the red light on top slowly fading in and out. Later on, they came up with much higher towers that used white strobe lights, but these red lamps were extremely lazy, as if the Texas summer heat slowed them down just like the rest of us while trying to move. The nearest one had a barbwire fence around it, but the other one was free and clear and particularly inviting. Around the age of eleven or so, my friend Clay and I started sneaking out at night. We weren't up to any harm in particular, but just being out and unregulated when everyone else was asleep had its charm. It was also the only time the temperature was under ninety degrees. We used to go and hang out at the local AM radio station (KRZI) and we got to know all the DJs there. They were all very nice, and it's hard to believe now, but they allowed us to sit there in the control room with them, as long as we didn't talk while they were on the air. Sometimes they even let us choose the music to play. Every time I hear "Band on the Run," "Radar Love," or "Come Monday," I immediately think about us walking around in the cool night air. We often timed our arrival at the nearby 7-Eleven to coincide with the delivery of fresh, hot honey buns around four o'clock a.m.

We eventually set our sights on that one unprotected tower and started climbing it. I think this one in particular was about five hundred feet high, and though we often didn't reach the top, it was still a very dangerous thing to do. Thinking about looking down from three hundred feet and seeing the tower disappear into the black void beneath sends shivers up my spine now. We reached the top twice and the last twenty feet to that hypnotic red light was only reached on the outside of the tower frame; the interior ladder just stopped. It was bad enough to climb that high in the dark, where the top climber could have slipped and taken both of us out, but at least we had something behind us, even if it was just the illusion of safety. We did have one last chance to grab something before falling. But to make that move to the outer frame where there was nothing but empty black space behind us…!

One night, I was in the lead. At each intersection and change of section color, there's a sort of small triangular platform that the ladder climbed through. It's not big enough to sit on and rest — at least for a human. About two-thirds of the way up, I passed one of those intersections and when my head came level with the platform, something squawked and took flight.

I nearly let go.

I'm sure the bird was equally surprised while sitting on her nest to suddenly see me at that height, but at least when she jumped, she had wings! That was the closest we came to tragedy while climbing radio towers. That whole experience would become a recurring nightmare later on. I would almost be to the top when it would suddenly take off like a rocket. Unfortunately, it would never quite reach orbit and then I would be hurled back to the earth at a horrible backward, upside-down angle. It's often been said that if you hit the ground in a dream, you'll really die. I can tell you that is not true. I landed in the bowling alley parking lot across from the tower many times in those dreams, and though it physically hurt for real because of my muscular contraction on impact, I survived.

After all that danger and effort, I didn't have anything to show for it, so on the second ascent, I availed myself of one of my sister's coats that was in our garage. The next day, she was graciously driving me somewhere when I looked up at the tower as we passed it — to see her coat gently swinging in the breeze at the top. I've since confessed that loving deed to her.

New Lows

Now that I think about it, I also remember hanging a lemon from one of my coiled guitar cords as a favor to a good friend, Elizabeth Lehman, from somewhere near the top. Enough of my towers stories, but I often wonder what might've happened to me without my family's prayers. There are many other situations where I could easily have died, but didn't for some reason. Like the time I met another car coming from the other direction on a one-lane bridge when we were both doing sixty to seventy miles an hour. I think we both saw the other one coming from far away and sped up to get across the bridge first. Instead, we met right in the middle and I scraped sides with both the passing car and the guard rail, and took out both side mirrors. One or two inches difference in either direction might have ended our lives.

Later, as a teen, I was walking through Cameron Park with a good friend and without really intending to, we began to climb one of the cliffs without any equipment. By the time we stopped talking and realized how far up we were, it really only made sense to continue to the top because it's usually more dangerous to descend. At some point, we separated on the face and I came to a place where there were no more handholds. I was perched on a tiny ledge and there was nowhere for me to go. There was a small root above me about the thickness of my index finger that curled out of the face, but it was a few inches above my outreached hands. I was probably a hundred feet above the ground and I realized for the first time that I might die that day. How could I have been so careless and stupid to place my life on the line like that for no good reason? It felt so selfish as I realized how I was about to impact my family and friends for something as senseless as that. I was going to have to jump and grab that root and it would either hold me or I would plummet to my death. I couldn't even bring myself to pray for rescue because it seemed so foolish for me to be up there in the first place. I simply said, "God, my life is in Your hands. If You want me to live, then I will. I'm so sorry that I did this to my family and if I do live, I will never do anything like this again." I don't judge those who rock climb and are trained and use good protective equipment and techniques, but I made a promise that day and have kept true to it.

Even though I was a Christian from the time I was eight years old, I was about to enter a whole new era of growth and maturity that I never could have anticipated.

Chapter 7

Divergent

One stone can change the course of a river, it's been said. I know this to be true from personal experience. A snowball could theoretically grow into a major avalanche. Certainly a small slide can quickly become a major force of destruction as it races down a mountainside and changes the geography forever.

My preschool experience began much like everyone else's: exciting, but scary as hell! I remember my first day in kindergarten as I sat there looking up at the alphabet and thinking, "Oh, I'm in way over my head...." I also have a candid memory of the refreshment cart coming in later that morning and the attending lady asking if there was anyone who was allergic to chocolate milk. I immediately raised my hand, thinking that "allergic" meant "really like." For days, I watched as that mysterious nectar of the cow was given to everyone but me. How could this be?? What had I done that I should be punished and singled out to miss such a delicious treat?

School Lesson 1: Pretending or assuming you know something you don't can lead to dire consequences!

I don't remember how that misunderstanding was finally worked out, but I drank dark moo-juice with vengeful abandonment for the rest of that year. I must have learned that lesson well because later in the third grade, I resisted the temptation to sign up and be included with a group of kids of whom I was truly envious. Every day, a teacher would come in and say, "Okay, everyone who signed up for Beach, come with me." I really wanted to go play at the beach, but something didn't seem quite right. I also couldn't figure out where it was, seeing that we were landlocked and all. Later in the year, I finally understood that the teacher was saying "Speech" and not "Beach." Either she was a poster child for that program or I needed to sign up for "Hearing Accurately" class.

Lens of Time

There's a peculiarity about time in that it not only softens pain, but it also has a filtering mechanism that tends to place an emphasis on certain aspects of your remembered life. When I look back at my youth, it seems like I never talked but only observed those around me. Even though I was shy, I know that wasn't true; I was just as talkative as other children, but I can't actually remember ever saying anything. I think that must be because I have always been sensitive to my environment and those around me, and this now leaves the mental impression that I only watched and observed others instead of engaging. Sort of like cerebral cream rising to the top.

I really was shy but I didn't have any trouble making friends. It seemed to come pretty easily for me and I wonder if that was because I had an interest in so many other things, I wasn't yet self-conscious enough to make friendship awkward.

Authentic friendship always begins with mutual enjoyment of an outside object or activity, and affection naturally grows without either of you being aware of it. It's only when you focus on each other too much and start playing the "Are we each other's best friend?" game that it can start the onset of self-doubt. Even as adults, I see too many people monitoring themselves to see if there is self-improvement or growth taking place. I think that is self-defeating beyond a certain point. Remember as a child how you used to sit up late on Christmas Eve waiting for Santa to arrive? Your very presence and attention actually prevented what you wanted most to happen! I believe true growth takes place when you're paying the least amount of attention to it.

I always did pretty well in my school work, getting A's and B's in everything except penmanship. I never got anything higher than a C on that, and I still suck when it comes to handwriting. It doesn't help when you're married to someone who has absolutely beautiful handwriting — even when signing those awkward credit card machines in stores. If signatures indicated your vocation, I would have been a doctor.

My favorite subjects were math and science, and I was even good at spelling at that time — I would usually be one of the last survivors in our local spelling bees. All that changed after I suffered a serious head injury at the age of forty. Not only did I completely lose my sense of taste and smell, I also became claustrophobic for a year and had trouble spelling even relatively simple words. You don't think about the mental process of spelling as you write until you can no longer do it. No one sits and thinks about grammatical rules and such; you "picture" the words in your mind and write from those images.

I know that sounds strange, but try it now and test it. It can kind of screw with your mind after a while, like asking a centipede which leg comes after which. It did just fine until you raised the question!

I could no longer "see" words and had to spell check a lot, which was very disturbing and bothersome. It took time to get over that disadvantage and I'm most of the way back, but I don't think I'll ever return to where I was before my skull fracture. It's the same with my sense of smell: it's maybe eighty or ninety percent normal even fourteen years later. Age is probably taking its toll, too, so it's hard to tell with any certainty how my recovery went before normal degradation took over.

It Begins…

Somewhere in the fifth grade, the snow slab began to move underneath me. I honestly don't remember if I got sick or something else happened, but I think that's likely as I often had respiratory illnesses back then. I missed enough time and I fell so far behind that a chain reaction began. I dreaded going back, which made me miss more school and fall even further behind. My grandmother helped me so much through her teaching background and knowledge, but that was way before home schooling became acceptable in the eyes of society and the school system. Truant officers began visiting us to see what was going on and pressured my mother to get me back into the system. She tried but I wasn't participating.

The snowball effect was quickly overtaking me and compounding the problem, and my mind began to close to the possibility of returning to public school. This became so distressing to my mother in particular because the pressure of running a household and working a full-time job was hard enough; trying to figure out what was going on and help me recover quickly became overwhelming. She probably could have forced me to return but she simply didn't have the energy, and her compassion also played a part. I was becoming increasingly sad and isolated as I struggled to figure out what was wrong with me, and was simultaneously dealing with the guilt from seeing what I was causing my family to go through. This also happened right at the time when social activities like parties and dances were starting to develop, and I was missing out on all of them. I certainly wasn't in an analytical frame of mind at the time, but it felt like all my friends were running along together and I had tripped and fallen down. A few looked back in sympathy but still kept running on ahead. Most didn't notice or look back at all, at least as I perceived it. The truth is, my classmates simply thought we had moved away or I had changed schools; but from my perspective, I felt abandoned.

Perception about yourself and situations can be so damaging because it's often totally wrong. You end up feeling a certain way about yourself or others and make decisions that are based on error. At that age, probably no one has the maturity or insight to sit down and talk about it and find out the truth. If you tried, they might just throw a mud pie at you and run away. The sad part is that even when you grow up, it's far too rare for people to reach out and express their feelings or concern, and so for different reasons (pride?), a misunderstanding can take place and separate friends. Who knows what we might miss out on because we never check to see if what we're feeling is accurate?

The Off Ramp

I became more lonely and desperate as all my friends left me far behind in school and social activities. Those who did keep in touch would come by to talk about problems they were having with a girlfriend or their family and I would listen and offer my advice. They usually felt better and thanked me with total sincerity, and then returned to their normal world without inviting me along. I was very happy to help those who came by, but I started to feel a little used and resentful after a while. I started picturing myself in a dark alley where people would secretly dive in to see me for a couple of hours of therapy and then quickly return to the land of the living, leaving me to remain in that dark place.

Where was my faith and relationship to God during this time? I honestly can't remember thinking about it much because I was falling deeper and deeper into despair and that's where my attention was fixed. I clearly remember one night when I was twelve, sitting in front of my gas stove and seriously thinking about taking my life. There was no way out and I couldn't stand the hopelessness anymore. It made me so sad to think how my family would feel, but when you're in that state of darkness, projected remorse really can't reach you enough to change your mind; you just want out.

I finally began talking to God late that night in the most honest, desperate conversation I'd ever had with Him. It went something like, "God, are You really there? Do You really care about me and are You actually involved in my life in any meaningful way right now or did You just create me and are waiting for me at the end of this life? I need to know right now or I'll be coming to see You soon." There are people who will say that I generated the illusion of response in order to back up my belief system. They are dead wrong in that supposition. Anyone who's ever been that hopeless knows that the last thing you are vulnerable to is self-deception. I was so far beyond that, nothing but genuine, tangible experience and evidence could convince me of His existence and promise of personal intimacy. And that's exactly what I got. It wasn't a voice or vision but a peace and warmth that was unmistakable. I absolutely knew He cared and loved me and simultaneously how impossible it was for me to manufacture what I was feeling right then. I didn't have any answers about my situation or what would happen to me, but it didn't matter. When you feel His presence that strongly, you realize the unthinkable: He is somehow the complete answer. It doesn't make any sense from the outside, but it's true and life-changing when you experience it.

Intercession

What I didn't know at the time was that my precious grandmother was on her knees, praying for me with an outpouring of tears and heart-wrenching concern about what would happen to me in life if I missed out on an education. Remember the covenant I mentioned at the end of the third chapter? She was interceding on my behalf in a way that was on a whole different level based on her piercing love for me and deep relationship to the Lord. I don't know exactly when this occurred, but she might have stayed there all night until she got an answer, when she suddenly felt a warm hand on her shoulder. She said she actually turned around to see if my mother had come in, and then realized Who's hand it was. She heard a voice tell her that I would be okay, that His hand was on me. She instantly stopped crying and went to bed in complete peace and slept without an ounce of care. I believe there was a covenant made that night because of her amazing love for me, and that is the reason why I've been protected throughout my life when I should have borne the consequences of my rebellion and bad choices. It's not amnesty by any means, but I truly believe something real happened between them in the form of a covenant, that I won't fully know or understand until I get Home.

As I began to earnestly read the Bible for the first time and talk to Him daily, I asked Him to be my Father and teach me how to become a man since I didn't have any role models to help me. I didn't understand until enough time was behind me, but what had felt like being a broken down car on the side of the road, abandoned and rusting away, was in reality Him taking me aside so He could rebuild me from the ground up before I reentered the highway of life at breakneck speed via music. And those feelings of being used by my friends? I began to understand that I was actually in training and being prepared for a purpose later in life when I would need the practiced skill of listening.

I was spending most of my time in the New Testament, Psalms and Proverbs and I ran across Psalm 40:1-3. This became my life verse: "I waited patiently for the Lord, and He inclined to me and heard my cry. He brought me up out of the pit of destruction; out of the miry clay, and He set my feet upon a rock making my footsteps firm. He put a new song in my mouth, a song of praise to our God. Many will see and revere and will trust in the Lord" (Ps. 40:1-3 NASB).

The songs would come later, and I can't speak of the many who would see and have awe for God because of me and my rescue, but I can say this: anything I am now, anything I have done or can do is because of Christ alone. Jesus has enabled me to write music without being able to read it and without having any knowledge of theory; to design and build my own home; to understand cosmology and physics on an intuitive level. None of this would have been possible without the regeneration of my heart and mind from His Spirit. I was lost and hopeless and ready to leave this world until I turned to Him with the complete submission of my life. Everything from there is a testimony to His faithfulness and to my restoration.

Changed and Unchanged

Though my inner torment was now over, my outer circumstances still remained and I continued to try to find my way back into public school. I was able to keep up enough to rejoin my classmates in junior high and actually got straight A's in seventh grade. But something had changed inside me and I now had a hard time concentrating in that structured class environment. I eventually quit school in tenth grade and found a full-time job working at the bowling alley, where I had already been in a league for several years. It was such a relief to finally be old enough to be allowed that decision, and so I never finished high school. I was in the work force and very happy to be there. For several years, I would continue to feel a disconnect with those my age who went on to college and pursued professional careers, but I was developing a new sense of identity and self-worth in Christ that didn't depend on social status and degrees.

I was "Divergent" but growing into a man with daily, intimate help from the One who made me.

It's important to note that there was a time later on when I was dating someone who went to Baylor University, and whose father was a professor there, that I prayed about getting my GED. Only you and God can know when you're honestly available and open to something like that, and I know I truly was. If I had felt Him leading me that way, I really would have obeyed, but I didn't feel that. I felt that my motive would've been entirely wrong and misplaced; that I would've only been doing it to impress and satisfy someone else's requirement for value. That's always wrong. You might as well try driving forward and steering by looking in the rearview mirror to see if you're still on the road. If you live that way, you will always be looking back to see who approved of your decision and direction — and ultimately — your self-worth.

Would I ever encourage someone else to quit school? Never! It will only make their journey through this life much harder than it needs to be. Imagine buying a complex machine and choosing not to read the manual; you can eventually figure out how it works, but it will take a lot longer to get there. The normal path of high school and college provides opportunities that won't easily happen otherwise. That being said, your life is not over if circumstances don't allow you to finish school for some reason. God can overcome anything if you look to Him for help.

Chapter 8

Starlight, Starbright

Two other great blessings had already taken root in my young life and now began to integrate themselves into my new walk with God: music and astronomy. Music was so revolutionary, it deserves its own space in the next chapter.

I had received a telescope for Christmas when I was eleven and it's hard to describe how excited I was as I began my own personal discovery of the stars and planets. I couldn't wait for the sun to finally set so I could get my first view of the night sky! We assembled the department store refractor, which was the standard 60 mm model. As I impatiently waited, I pored over the star chart I also got that morning and dreamed of what the first star would look like. Saturn was also high on my list of objects to see. Would that stupid sun ever go down??

As the forgiving sun finally set, I set up my scope on our front porch and stared into the increasingly indigo sky for any sign of a star or planet, when I suddenly saw something very faint. I trained my sight on it and held my breath in anticipation. There it was, centered in the eyepiece. I quickly changed to a higher magnification and refocused. It was brighter but still only a pinpoint of light. I discovered the reality that stars are so far away that no magnification can ever resolve any star into a disc. What held me in complete fascination though, was the rapidly changing colors I saw in the brightest stars, especially Sirius. I was so impressed and proud of my new telescope and the kaleidoscope of flashing colors that it brought to me. I didn't realize until later that it was my inferior optics that created all the false colors I was seeing.

Let the baby have his bottle. I was damned excited with everything I was seeing and experiencing, and my love for the star-filled night sky was turning onto a passion that would never leave me. I have to confess some disappointment when reading Revelation 22:5 back then, that there wouldn't be a sun or moon, or even night anymore in Heaven. It's actually a wonderful, comforting insight into our future life for many reasons, but I didn't like to think about not seeing the stars. I don't really believe that's true now; when we're in our immortal bodies, I think we'll have access to His creation in ways that are beyond our present imagination.

Solitary Celebration

For the next week, I spent every sunless moment I could under that enchanting night sky that looked like diamond dust thrown onto black velvet. I soon found my way around using my chart and discovered planets, open clusters, and the most visible nebulae. What eluded me for two weeks was Saturn. That has to be on the top of everyone's list as a newbie, but I just couldn't locate it! Finally, one night I was out enjoying the sky with my naked eyes when I noticed one object that wasn't twinkling and that had a slightly orangish tint. I quickly grew excited about the possibility but didn't want to get my hopes up too high. I ran into our house, brought my scope out, and set it up. I'll never forget the moment the object swam into the field of view and the feeling of astonishment I felt as I focused, and the oblong thingy resolved itself into rings. I couldn't believe how glorious it looked and I ran around our yard silently screaming and jumping into the air!

There are certain moments in life that stand totally apart; that was one of them. For all the wonders up there, nothing could touch that one. Seeing globular clusters and the Great Red Spot on Jupiter, along with finding the Andromeda Galaxy came close, but my first sight of Saturn in a telescope was a singular moment. Stargazing is a perfect environment to talk to God. It's totally silent, but with a majesty that almost shouts. I feel the same sensation even now when I see a falling star. The amount of kinetic energy taking place right before your eyes as it burns up is so breathtaking, you can almost hear it.

When Two Become One

My nightly sojourn before the heavens was also my prayer time and they became synonymous with each other. The wonder of reading about Christ in the Bible, coupled with what I was seeing in His handiwork above, began a work of foundation building inside me and would soon protect me from believing lies and deceptions about happiness and identity. My first sip of American beer came during one of our block parties as a child and I couldn't stand the taste of it. Give me a Dr Pepper or Big Red any day, but not this! Why would any kid or teenager drink it except to appear more grown up? It just didn't interest me in any way, and it would be another thirty-four years before I would actually find enjoyment in a beer. It happened in a pub in Ireland. I started to like beer when Laura and I first shared a pint of Guinness. That's the only brand I'll drink now if I'm in a bar or when my good friend, Mark Trofholz, comes over to watch a movie. I enjoyed some mixed drinks along the way, especially Pina Coladas. Wine became a favorite, too, but only after I acquired a taste for it.

If you're completely honest, every form of alcohol is pretty nasty when you first taste it; it's really only a decision to persevere that allows you to eventually find pleasure in it. I enjoy drinking single malt scotch now, mostly because of our experience in Ireland and the incredible history behind it. Maybe it's just my particular taste buds that prevent me from liking most brands of beer, because I also don't like most kinds of cheese. It's almost unheard of for any kid not to like grilled cheese sandwiches, but there you are. I've said it before and I'll say it again: if you tasted cheese the way I taste cheese, you wouldn't eat it either.

It was still a time of loneliness as I explored the skies but I was never alone like I was before, and never would be again. It's really hard for me to understand and express what was changing inside me during this time, and because of this, I again wonder if that is because I was not really even thinking about it. I was too busy learning about Him and exploring His creation. I can't help but believe that we are happiest when we're not thinking about ourselves. Of course, we are always aware of what we're feeling and how we relate to others and they to us, but I was slowly coming to a place where my self-worth was no longer directly dependent on what other people thought of me. I was certainly coming to the firm realization that someone's true identity and personality had absolutely nothing to do with alcohol and getting drunk. In fact, it was the opposite as I saw it. My friends were already great people, but they quickly lost appeal and any edge they had the more they drank. I don't know the exact age when this thought first occurred to me, but I remember thinking that if you really felt like you could only be funny and likable after drinking, something was seriously wrong.

A Cord of Three Strands

Another indication of how I was growing happened as new friends were beginning to trickle back into my life. I would imagine everyone experiences some form of jealousy, even in friendship. When three people become friends, it's easy to start wondering how much you mean to someone and where you stand in their affection compared to the third person. The tendency is to imagine a sort of King of the Hill scenario, where there's only room for one to stand supreme above all the others. During one such struggle when I was fourteen, I experienced such an epiphany that I have no doubt where it came from. I believe the Lord showed me that I was completely wrong in how I perceived relative value and friendship. It's not relative at all but absolute. Let me explain: the human heart is not like a hill where only one may stand; instead, it has many chambers and each one is unique to a single person. So there's no need for competition because no one else can fit in your place, nor you in theirs. That's why it's absolute instead of relative; it has nothing to do with anyone else, but only with that person. This revolutionized my whole concept of friendship, and indeed any relationship. I will never forget those lessons.

Anytime the Lord speaks into your life, it brings about liberty and freedom from something. Simple truth. That doesn't mean that it will be easy, because the good He intends for us doesn't always line up with our understanding or our desires. So the real question becomes, what are you going to do when His guidance directly contradicts your intention? If I had chosen, I could have argued the strategies for keeping my imaginary "Hill" and remained in bondage. Instead, I chose to trust Him and activate that truth in my mind, and that common battle has remained almost nonexistent throughout my life since. I just wish I had the wisdom to always trust Him in every area of my life because of His proven faithfulness, but it seems like I have always withheld at least one area at any given time that I was unwilling to give up.

Another clarifying truth came to me at that time — a truth that has helped my walk with God. One day, while listening to other believers debate and argue about theological issues, it occurred to me to ask the question: what difference would it make in your life the next morning in how you live and relate to people? It's such a simple question, but it's beautifully disarming regarding a complexity that could otherwise just leave you confused. Sometimes it helps to reduce something down to a practical situation, where it can reveal its true nature and impact on others. Jesus said that we will know false teachers by their fruit, but it's also true of our actions, and even vague concepts fall prey to and reveal their true nature under that honest light. What would be the result of a certain belief? How would it line up against Jesus' commandment to love God above all other things and your neighbor as yourself?

Stars on Wheels

In my early twenties, I bought my first motorcycle and loved the feeling of freedom it gave me. I always wore a helmet but sometimes I would leave the visor up – that is, until I was riding on a country road and got hit in the eye by some kind of bug. It felt like a beetle and almost took my head off. The other hard-won lesson came as I was riding in Cameron Park with a friend while wearing shorts and a muscle shirt. I hit some gravel while going downhill at forty miles per hour and laid my motorcycle on its side, with me under it. That's the only time I was ever in deep pain and had time to wonder when it was going to stop; I just kept on sliding. I eventually stopped and immediately jumped up wondering if I still had my limbs intact. I was okay except for major road rash all the way up my left leg and arm. It really stung at the time but I think it was far worse when the scabs formed. Every time I stood up for the next two weeks, the blood would rush to those injuries and I felt like I would pass out. One day my grandmother affectionately told me to "get along" and then slapped me right on my leg scab. I had to lean on the dresser for a few minutes so I wouldn't black out after that one.

Being on my bike was so pleasurable and my rides often ended under dark skies where I could view the heavens, but I was about to encounter a situation where it became even more important to me. I mentioned in the last chapter that I had dated a girl at Baylor. I broke off the relationship after realizing we really weren't that well suited for each other, and also because I recognized that she was using me to fill a place in her life that only God should fill. It was a very unpleasant breakup and while I left with a very heavy heart, I was also determined not to make that same mistake myself, where I might place an unrealistic burden on someone else. I decided that night that I wouldn't date for a year and I would try to make sure that my self-worth was fulfilled in Christ alone and not in another human being. Of course, everywhere I went, I saw couples laughing and having fun together! I was still determined to remain single during that time and went into the country almost every night on my motorcycle to talk to God and enjoy the stars. I was intrigued at the thought of what a relationship could be like if both people were already complete in their vertical relationship to God, and then came together. Seemed like it could be pretty amazing.

Heavenly Perspective

I'll never forget one of those outings. I saw something that I have never seen before. All the visible planets were spread out evenly across the sky. It was a very dark night and the Milky Way was also clearly visible. What this gave me was a perspective on how tilted our solar system plane is relative to our galaxy. If you hold out two pencils in front of you horizontally, and then tilt each one slightly, that gives you some idea. I don't know the exact amount, but it may be as much as twenty degrees askew. (Okay, I just checked and it is sixty degrees off parallel!) I guess this really doesn't have a point, except that I had never heard that before and was completely caught off guard when I saw it that way.

Another memorable experience came when Lee Ann and I were driving toward Cuchara, Colorado. There were no city lights around us at all and the sky was darker and more stable then I have ever seen it. I had to stop the car and get out and I couldn't believe my eyes. I had trouble recognizing a single constellation because there were so many stars visible! None of them were shimmering in the slightest so the atmosphere had to be about as stable as it could possibly be.

I still love to go out on our balcony and look at the stars. There's a peace that I can't find anywhere else except under the night sky. It may be because of my history and walk with the Creator during my troubled teen years and all that took place within me, or maybe it's just built into His creation and everyone feels it who will sit still long enough for it to soak into them.

My love of astronomy at that particular time perhaps taught me that public school is only one way to learn, that there is no limit on how much you can learn on your own. I didn't think about it at the time, but God was covertly instilling a new confidence into me regarding my own intelligence and desire to pursue higher education in my own way. I now have an insatiable appetite for it! Both my mother and grandmother always encouraged me and validated who I was, but there was something Grace used to say when I got discouraged that really stuck with me: "You were born intelligent." I knew she really meant it and that helped me so much in those formative years.

Chapter 9

The Language of Music

If for no other reason in the wide world, I would believe there's a Creator because of music. In my mind, there's no other possible explanation for something so obviously outside ourselves. If you lived in a home without doors or windows, but heard wonderful sounds and smelled tantalizing scents coming from beyond the walls, you would conclude there had to be another world outside your own home, even if you couldn't see it yet with your own eyes. Music is a language that surpasses all human language and shouts that there is something more magnificent and larger than what we can see with our human eyes. It's universal and doesn't require knowledge or training to understand how it makes you feel inside. It's right there from the start. I believe it's here to give us incredible pleasure now, but also to lead us Home.

As I mentioned before, my mother was a wonderful musician who could both read sheet music and play by ear. She never got into composing on a serious level, though she had a couple of songs she played around with from time to time. In addition to piano, she also played accordion and guitar. She never approached me about learning any of them, but my own curiosity took hold regarding both the guitar and piano.

Curiosity Becomes Purpose

I was probably around the age of ten or eleven when I first picked up my mother's acoustic guitar and began to explore it, and soon found that I could pick out melodies that I heard on the radio. There must have been a Mel Bay book around because I started working on chords and how to hold the "plectrum" or guitar pick. The included sample songs were horrendous! The Beatles were far more interesting and challenging, but I didn't know enough yet to do anything but play the melodies. I eventually learned a few chords from Mr. Bay, when my mother discovered that I was playing it upside down. In her casual way, she merely suggested that I turn it over because I'm right handed and it might lead to problems later on if I didn't. She obviously wasn't familiar with Jimi Hendrix — but neither was I at that time.

How could I start all over?? I already knew three chords! I finally gave in and turned it over and tried to adapt to this totally alien way of playing guitar. The guitar itself was about the worst thing I could have started with. I don't even think it had a name on it and I don't know where it came from either; probably purchased somewhere overseas while my parents were still married. The action was terrible which made it very hard to press the strings down cleanly. It should have discouraged me and probably would have been to the more casual student, but once I set my eyes on a goal, I usually stayed after it. The other problem was that the plastic surrounding the tuning gears started to crack and break off after getting this much frequent attention after so long (she rarely played it). I can't even begin to guess how old the strings were at that time. I know they had a fine coating of rust and it felt like they might slice my fingers open when I ran them up and down the first and second strings. Not good.

It didn't seem to stop me, however, and I used a pair of pliers to tune the gears that were broken. We should have changed the strings, but we didn't. Maybe we were afraid the strings might be the only thing still holding the guitar together. I worked my way through the basic open chords that sounded nice to me and didn't worry about the rest. It's funny how you already have opinions, even when you're that young, about what you like and don't like. I didn't like major seventh chords. I still don't. I refer to them as "laxative chords" now. I guess it's how you use them because Pink Floyd's "Breathe" and "Time" went a long way in healing my ugly bias and opened my mind to their possible use and justification for existence. There, I said it.

You Are What You Hear

I don't remember seeing The Beatles on Ed Sullivan (I would have been three) but our mom bought us *Meet the Beatles* a couple of years later, either in '66 or '67. I know it had to be around that time because I spent hours listening to it and singing along while pretending that I was singing to my first girlfriend in second grade. I only remember that her first name was Tonya and that we used to spend recess writing messages on the chalk board right in front of each other. How's that for a pair of shy extraverts? We couldn't say it but we could write it. My only other memory of Tonya is shopping for shoes at Lewis Shoe Store in Lake Air Mall and then going to eat at an indoor diner nearby. She was sitting in a booth with her family and I passed her trying to look cool while holding on to my mom with one hand and the golden egg I received from the shoe store in the other. A pretty unrealistic goal.

That Beatles album also started my amateur dart career. Four white faces on a black background? I mean, be fair! What else could you expect from a six-year-old? Pretty soon they were covered with tiny holes as I valiantly tried to hit each one in the eye. We probably could have gotten a lot of money for that cover, but it was sacrificed to my attempt at being World Champion Dart Thrower, which subsequently ended the next year. Among the many great songs on that album, "That Boy" in particular touched me deeply with its unusual harmonies. Very haunting.

I don't think I was dedicated enough yet to really learn the guitar until I first heard ZZ Top and Bachman-Turner Overdrive. That electric guitar sound was amazing and I had to have it! My mother took me to a pawnshop where I asked to play one. I could barely stand the excitement as the sales clerk started setting everything up. He hung it around my neck and I accidentally hit a string before he even had the amp turned on and instantly I knew it was wrong. I didn't know the difference between bass and lead until that moment. I was so disappointed (sorry, bass players!).

Zeppelinized

Something else happened when I was eleven that would change me forever. I heard "Stairway to Heaven" on the radio and wanted to buy the album it was on, so off we went to Clark's Department Store in search of it. That one was out of stock so I settled for *Led Zeppelin*, their first release. It was a fall day when I put that eight-track on and heard the opening chords to "Good Times, Bad Times," and I was instantly undone. I had never heard anything like that in my life. The sheer power from Jimmy Page's guitar was breathtaking on those chords and riffs. I later came to know many cool girls who loved that band, too, but I have to say that distorted electric guitar was made for teenage boys. The energy and adrenaline is a perfect match for our nature at that age.

That did it! It was time to get an electric guitar. Another visit to a pawnshop, and this time, it was the right species of instrument. A Fender Mustang was in my hands and screaming to be ridden hard! The price was too high and I sadly put it back as we walked toward the door, talking about possibly selling my minibike to get the money. The owner overheard us and called us back from the front door. He said he was looking for a minibike for one of his kids for Christmas, and so we made the deal.

Now I had a real instrument and could set aside that wooden torture device that was my acoustic. I still didn't have an amp, so I couldn't create those enormous sounds I was hearing, but I was getting closer. I could at least start learning those incredible songs and was on my way to developing my ear for hearing things and knowing how to play them that has served me my entire life. I didn't know I was playing by ear or that such a term existed, and that's because when you have such a strong passion about something, you don't even think about such technicalities and terms. You just run as fast as your little legs can carry you until you find your limit.

Relativity

I honestly believe that is the fundamental difference between being young and feeling old later. Youth always looks ahead toward possibilities and new discoveries, and it's only when you first start looking back that the age clock starts ticking. The young always reach for more and there are all kinds of landmarks ahead of you, such as first becoming a teenager, then getting your driver's license, turning eighteen, etc. The list goes on and on. But at some point — usually in your thirties — you start reminiscing and looking back at your youth and wishing you could experience some of those things again. That's wonderful in and of itself and there's incredible pleasure and purpose in looking back over your life experiences. The problem comes when you stop listening to new music and exploring the world at large. That's when you really do start growing old. Beware, lest you look back too much and allow your life to become a living museum. As long as you have breath, there's adventure awaiting you. When you do finally breathe your last, the next adventure is simply staggering.

In our late thirties, a very good friend of mine and I would sometimes meet people within a few years of our own age, but there was all the difference in the world between us. We tried to quantify it, and though having children was probably a big part of that equation, there was still something more troubling. They just stopped living and learning. We began to see certain people, look at each other and say, "The adventure's over." That phrase really captured what we were feeling and the sadness we felt for them. They were no longer open to new experiences in whatever form they might come.

We all know now that time is relative and stretchable — even a physical part of space itself — and though we will all be beyond time after we die, we still have to deal with it as a reality here. So here's my hypothesis: when you lean forward expectantly, time is stretched and you feel as though you have endless amounts of it. When you lean back and plant your feet, time is compressed and it forces you forward, even against your will. So keep on living as though you are eternal (which I absolutely believe we all are) and never stop growing, learning, and — most of all — having adventures. If C. S. Lewis is correct, then real life hasn't even begun yet.

Chapter 10

The On Ramp

My self-training now began in earnest, both regarding music and my life in general. The Lord was continuing to work on my mind and heart but I was also totally absorbed with learning to play guitar and discovering new music. My exposure was limited to AM radio at the time, and even though it provided a variety that can't be imagined today, it was still pretty much small potatoes compared with what was out there. I had bought several more Zep albums and they were now my favorite band. I hadn't yet made the all-important transition away from the infamous eight-track and had a pretty good collection of ZZ Top and B.T.O. plus a few others in that unfortunate format. I would later be teased about a statement I made saying that I wanted to have nothing but eight-tracks forever. You can pity me now.

A friend had come over for Halloween in 1975 and we walked around our extended neighborhood, just hanging out. As we headed onto a less familiar street nearby, my friend said he knew someone there and that we should stop by. I was introduced to Billy Haney and we went into his room to listen to music and talk. I was immediately confronted with a poster of Frank Zappa and several others that I had never seen before.

Billy had Leslie West and Mountain playing and I liked that okay and we really started hitting it off as we talked about music and playing guitar. He had a Sears SG knockoff and it looked great to me. Our mutual friend had discovered a book on Linda Lovelace and he was mentally absent for the rest of the evening. Billy switched to *Apostrophe* by Zappa and he didn't even notice and asked if it was still Leslie West playing. The strange thing is, Billy later said this guy had never come over before, and he never did again. It's as if his sole purpose that night was to introduce us and then move on.

Destiny

I must've mentioned that I worked at the bowling alley because Billy came there the next day looking for me. Everyone looks different in the daylight and in a new environment, so neither one of us was sure if we recognized the other one or not. We both had that look of, "Are you, *you?*" We finally made the connection and got together at his house again. He had so much more experience and knowledge about good music that I asked him what I should buy. We walked to a music store near us called Stereo Center and he recommended *Stand Up* by Jethro Tull and *Johnny Winter Captured Live*. I loved both of them and we began a lifelong friendship. Billy even showed me how to play my first bar chord and "Norwegian Wood" by the Beatles.

He introduced me to Yes and I infected him with my love for Zeppelin. In the summer we met almost every day to listen to some new album and then would go have lunch at the nearby Sonic Burger or Burger King. FM radio and album rock were really taking over the airwaves and Billy was so well versed in this world that was completely new to me. I found out B.T.O. was playing at Baylor and we got tickets, so that was my very first concert. Neither of us could drive yet, so my sister had to take us and pick us up in her Vega. Speaking of my sister, her room was right next to mine and I feel so bad now because she had to listen to my favorite songs over and over as I played along — for by now, I had my first amp. It was a Yamaha 2x12 100w solid-state that was loud! The distortion sounds were never that good but the clean sounds could knock your shirt off, especially when I played my Gibson double-neck through it later. That time period was probably the most stressful for our relationship, because we were always great friends. We still are and Lee Ann now lives only sixteen miles away in Estes Park, Colorado.

Live and in Person

One evening, Billy and I were walking through a record store when we both suddenly stopped dead in our tracks; somebody was playing a version of "Stairway to Heaven" that neither one of us had heard before. We ran to the counter to ask about it and discovered Zeppelin had a live double album called *The Song Remains the Same*. Of course, we both bought it immediately and heard performances like we'd never imagined. We watched *The Midnight Special* and Don Kirshner's *Rock Concert*, hoping to see someone good, and one night we did. They showed an excerpt from the film of the same name and it was coming to Waco in October 1976. Jimmy Page and Robert Plant were such visual mysteries, as were a lot of rock stars back then, so we didn't know what to expect. Neither one of us was prepared for the moment when the lights came on and they burst into "Rock and Roll." We sat there speechless and electrified by their stage presence and how they moved. No one else had ever looked that cool on stage. I still get chills when I see that opening song, as well as how Page moves while playing his double-neck on "The Song Remains the Same". He literally glides across the stage in some mysterious way during the first minute of the song. It's hard to express how much that film impacted me. Others around the world obviously felt something similar but everyone has their own story to tell.

April 1977 came with another special surprise. Zeppelin was coming to Dallas! Billy and I got tickets through a local station that included a bus ride to the show and back. How absolutely magical to see them live. It was thrilling for me to see Page's famous ZOSO cab and Orange amp in person.

I really found my niche in playing by ear and basically taught myself how to play guitar by learning every Zeppelin song I could. This opened huge vistas for me and I was suddenly thrown into a spotlight of sorts for being able to play this stuff that was so popular. Friends would bring their friends by so I could play for them in my room (poor Lee Ann). By the time I was sixteen, I had already learned the live version of "Dazed and Confused" note for note and was ready to perform it live. The opportunity came when I booked our band to play on the Dr Pepper stage at the Heart O' Texas Fair in Waco. I even borrowed a Marshall amp stack and authentic Echoplex, the same kind that Jimmy Page used. I already had my own violin bow, so we were ready to rock! A lot of my friends came out to see us and we were well into our set and things were going well. Then, we launched into "Dazed." I was playing the extended bow solo and was at the place when Page slaps it against his strings and it echoes back. Apparently, that was just too much for those in charge and they shut off the power to our stage. Show over.

My mother, who was there in the audience, overheard someone say that I was hurting my guitar. No explanation or apologies from the authorities, just darkness. I sat down in disbelief for a few minutes and then we packed up and went home. The worst thing was that it was our former next-door neighbor who threw the switch; the same guy who used to ogle my sister when she sunbathed in our backyard. I'm amazed this experience didn't stop me right then from wanting to play music anymore, but it didn't. I was too enthralled by the whole thing and couldn't wait to play again.

Have Outlet, Will Play

This we did every chance we got and it wasn't unheard of for us to get chased off by the police. Our philosophy was, "Have Outlet, Will Play," and that meant outdoor shopping malls or empty school properties were vulnerable to our musical needs and whims. We had some strange experiences while playing in Cameron Park at night when creepy people would just suddenly appear out of the darkness, complete with lightning flashes and thunder to add to the effect. Fortunately, they were harmless and just made for some great stories later. One dude was particularly scary, though. We didn't even hear him approach, we just looked up and there he was — huge and hairy. He wore what I can only describe as a traditional pimp hat, and everything about his demeanor spelled trouble for us young 'uns. By the end of the night, he was right up there beside us singing away, so no harm done. Another night, a woman showed up and stood there waiting to be entertained. We tried to explain that we were just there to rehearse and not to perform, to which she replied, "I don't care, just play da sh**!"

I was suddenly being invited to lots of parties and we sometimes played at them as well. This was when that new inner strength and personal identity came into play for the first time. Everyone around me was smoking pot and getting drunk and I wanted nothing to do with it. By this time, I knew that those things were empty and often just masked and diminished who my friends really were. The amazing thing is that no one — not one single person — ever teased me or harassed me when I would say no thanks and pass it on. It is such a testimony and tribute to the quality of my friends that they always accepted me even when I didn't participate in what they were doing. I also never looked down at them, either. I just wished they could see how much better they were without those things.

Lesson on the Lawn

There was one house party that I'll always remember. Most of the people there were already trashed, including most of my bandmates, so we took a break and I went outside and sat on their beautiful front lawn. A few minutes later, a very attractive girl came out and sat down beside me and told me how impressed she was that I didn't feel the need to get high; that I was okay with saying no and just enjoying life as it was. This blew my mind, especially coming from someone like her — smart, beautiful and popular. I couldn't believe she would even notice me in the first place, much less be observing me and then be impressed by anything I did. That was a huge lesson for me — I think the first of its kind. People really do notice what you say and do, whether they ever bring it to your attention or not. People notice.

We ended up dating for a couple of weeks and then recognized that we were somehow better suited as friends. It's one of the few times that such a mutual, natural transition occurred because far more often, it's awkward and one-sided. Julie and I have enjoyed a close friendship that's unique and very precious to each of us for several decades now. A few years ago, my wife and I went to stay with her at her home in St. Thomas. She became an orthopedic surgeon and is one of the most talented and accomplished people I've ever known. Her sensitivity and determination to come talk to me that night turned into an incredible life-long blessing for us both. It's something to think about the next time you are impressed with someone because of their character or the choices they've made. Go tell them.

I continued to progress in my playing and started to contemplate forming a band that played only Led Zeppelin. Tribute bands weren't that common yet but I knew it would be popular. I bought a cherry sunburst Les Paul Standard and then found a white Gibson double-neck and grabbed it. I would have preferred to have a red one but they weren't that common back then and custom orders were too expensive. I wasn't really trying to look like Page in every way, I just wanted to sound like him. I did adopt his unusual habit of hanging his guitar down to his knees. I couldn't find any strap that was long enough so I had to add a string extension to get it down there. This forced me to play bar chords by wrapping my thumb over the neck to press down the sixth string, which felt and looked so cool. I still often use this technique now even though I've since raised my strap to a mortal person's range. Eric Johnson later changed everyone's concept of finger placement and what was possible through stretching, and that certainly negated the low-slung guitar approach that was more common in the '70s. I probably would have developed a hump if I had kept playing that way much longer.

Press This!

The *Waco Tribune-Herald* got word of my plan and scheduled an interview. I don't want to name the journalist who came over that day, but it was a complete fiasco. He didn't record our conversation like he should have, but only took occasional notes and then went back and "recreated" the interview in his own style and vernacular. I was mortified when I read it. The picture he took turned out great, but every quote of me was twisted into unrecognizable garbage. I sounded like a complete buffoon by the sentence structure and words he used. They didn't even sound anything like me, but there they were in quotation marks and the result was that several friends, including the potential singer, were offended and we broke up. Even people I didn't know wrote in to the paper to express how ignorant I was according to the things I supposedly said. I was deeply hurt by that experience and forever afterward, I wouldn't agree to an interview unless it was recorded.

There were a lot of excellent musicians in Waco in the '70s and '80s, and I was privileged to record and play shows with many of them, even if that original tribute band idea didn't work out.

The sad thing is that I have always had bad luck with promoting and marketing myself. Material I send gets lost or they decide to replace my bio with their own description. I can't even count the number of times my carefully worded submittal was replaced with "Singer/Songwriter." First of all — I don't sing! I compose instrumental music. At least give the audience accurate and fair warning so they know what they're in for.

Chapter 11

Sound by Design

That whole experience left me with a bitter taste in my mouth and I dropped the idea of playing Zeppelin exclusively. Of course, the main reason was that I didn't know anyone who could pull off singing Robert Plant, Yes, Kansas, Queen, Rush or other bands I was into then. Much later, I would become good friends with an excellent musician who had that kind of range and an almost identical taste in music. His name is Steve Tindle and we played in the same worship band together at Rocky Mountain Church in Estes Park. Unfortunately, we didn't meet until we were in our early forties and way beyond doing that kind of thing anymore because of commitments and other interests. I sure wish I could have met him much sooner in life.

The title of this chapter is actually a double entendre, because not only did I become interested in sound design and synthesis, I was also now "sound by design" (relatively).

I composed my first song on our piano when I was nine. My grandmother was teaching Lee Ann how to play and read music and I'm sure the offer was extended to me, but I wasn't interested beyond throwing pencils at my sister. I got a little too close on one pass-through and got my one and only spanking from Grace. I should also mention that she pretended to call the orphanage once when we were in rare form. It worked.

Playing by Candlelight

I poked around on the keyboard and came up with several sections that I pieced together into one song. Because I had no idea what notes I was playing, I had to come up with a way to remember them. There was a candle nearby. Hmm...

I'll drip wax on each key that I play! Little did I know that hot wax isn't good for piano keys. Apparently, those keys weren't pure ivory and they melted anywhere my molten markers fell. Another lesson learned the hard way, but at least I knew how to play my song! And so did everyone else who ever played that piano — they just didn't know the order of the notes. This was way before music videos were even thought of, but I had visions of how my new song would look. The observer would be out in the ocean at twilight. As soon as the first notes played, an island would begin to be drawn at an accelerated pace a little distance away. Then, when it was finished, the viewer would immediately begin to move across the water toward the island and eventually start slowing as you moved across the beach and into the trees. All this was represented by the music and tempo changes, with the final destination taking place when you suddenly came to a clearing in the center of the island. There, you found a beautiful waterfall and refreshment from the tropical heat. Computer animation would have been perfect for that.

The song became "Secret Garden" on my *World of Colors* CD. That original vision still works, but my time with the Lord under the stars came to represent a more complete vision for it and I adapted the arrangement accordingly. If you remember, I had quit going to church with my mother and it wasn't until I found another church in my late teens that I started going again on a consistent basis. This was Highland Baptist and it was an amazing experience, something I hadn't seen the likes of before. There were between 2,500 and 3,000 people attending and they were mostly in their twenties and thirties. With three Sunday morning services and two in the evening, you had endless opportunities to meet new people your age. This place was alive and growing and I wanted to be a part of it! I don't know who first invited me but it was another turning point in my walk with Christ. This was about the same time I had broken up with my Baylor girlfriend and had started riding my motorcycle in the country on most nights to be alone with the Lord. It was such an important growth period for me because I was learning how to hear His voice and not just offer up prayers in a one-way communication.

The Voice Within

If any Christian is honest, that isn't easily done at first. This is totally different from reading the Bible and learning His will and general direction for everyone. It should begin that way and it's foundational, but this is learning to be quiet in your spirit and allow His gentle voice to speak directly into your life and situation. First of all, your mind chatters endlessly and you have to constantly rein it in. That is a difficult discipline in itself, and then you have to discern His voice from your own consciousness. Again, not so easy to do at first. I often hear Christians say that God told them this and He told them that or to put on pink socks that morning. This has always bothered me, because it leaves everyone around them feeling like something must be wrong with them. I've never heard explicit directions while dressing and usually end up with different colored socks anyway. I'm not saying that some people don't have a deep and personal relationship with Him or doubt that they can easily hear His voice now, but I think it's misleading to say it with such casualness and flippancy. To be perfectly honest, it has often troubled me why His voice has to be so quiet and subtle. This I do know from experience: the more you obey what you do hear, the easier it gets.

So, how do you know if it's His voice you're hearing? Well, what would it produce if you followed it? He won't ever tell you to hurt anyone and it won't go against His written word. That's why it's so important to read the Bible and understand His nature and heart for all of us. Here's an example before I return to the subject of music. One of the very first things I asked Him during that period of purposeful prayer was if there was anything in my life that He wanted to change. Very simple and practical. As I waited to hear something, I felt like the answer that came into my mind was about gossip. I worked for a company that was rife with it. At first I wondered if I was really hearing His voice, but it was such a good thing to do anyway, I decided to go with it and try to distance myself from it the next day. I never initiated gossip but I certainly participated in it. The next night, I talked to Him about how I had done and felt such a peace in return. It was a good lesson and confirmation. It also instilled a confidence in my reciprocal relationship with God that would build. I'll go into more detail later.

Synthesis

Even though guitar was my main instrument, it might have been partly due to bands such as Yes and Genesis that I became increasingly aware of what keyboardists were playing. Their sound was often the key ingredient to the power and mood of many of my favorite songs. How were they getting those sounds? Outside of the venerable B3 and electric piano, there was something much more exciting going on and it all had to do with the still relatively new synthesizer. Search engines didn't exist yet, but music magazines such as *Circus* and *Cream* provided enough images to know that modular Moogs (sounds like "modes," not "moods") were part of the keyboardist's arsenal, but I also knew I could never afford those gigantic and untamable beasts. A local store had a much smaller synth that I was looking into. It so happened that it was Yamaha's very first entry into the synth market, called the SY-1. You could only play one note at a time (monophonic) and they used pre-programmed "sound tabs" for your basic timbres, along with a few sliders to adjust other parameters such as attack, decay, sustain and release (ADSR), and filter cutoff, etc. An amazing feature, especially so early in analog technology, was that it had "aftertouch," meaning you could add vibration or brightness by pressing the key down harder after you played it. It was enough for me and I bought it in 1977, when I was sixteen. This allowed our band to play songs that had prominent synth solos in them such as "Never Been Any Reason" by Head East, "Lucky Man" by ELP, "Fragile" by Yes, and "Magic Man" by Heart among many others.

I was very intrigued with the sounds I was getting and wanted to explore this new world of sound creation. You can only do so much with a mono synth, so I started setting my sights on bigger and better keyboards as they developed them and became more affordable. Digital sound generation revolutionized the industry around 1978, but they were more expensive than your house. A few years later, I was on a date at a great jazz club in Dallas called Strictly Tabu when I saw the keyboardist playing something I hadn't seen before. This synthesizer was polyphonic and sounded fantastic! It was a six-voice Memorymoog and you could store one hundred of your own sounds in its internal memory. When the band took a break, the keyboardist left it in test mode, where all the LEDs sequenced and flashed in a rapturous pattern of tech delight. Oh, I had to have one! I bought mine in 1982 and devoted all my time to learning and creating various soundscapes and timbres. Each voice had three VCOs or oscillators and it was incredibly rich — especially when you set it to "Unison" mode. All eighteen VCOs played together, and you had better have turned down the volume beforehand! Amazing beastie. There were two downsides to it: analog was notoriously hard to keep in tune because it tended to drift as the electronics heated up. Fortunately, they had a great feature called AutoTune, and that worked well. The other problem was when I bought it. A year later someone invented MIDI (Musical Instrument Digital Interface), a software and hardware interface that allowed an extraordinary amount of control over all the parameters and actual remote performances later on. I could have added the available conversion kit, but it was ridiculously expensive.

Frailty, Thy Name Is Analog

This new instrument opened a whole world of opportunities for recording and performing with other musicians. I recorded an entire album with an artist playing nothing but keyboards — no guitar at all. She was in Waco for a short time competing in the Miss Texas pageant and we hit it off immediately. I would play racquetball with her boyfriend in the mornings and then compose and record all day and evening with her at Sound Arts studio. I don't know whatever happened with that album but it was a wonderful experience and really fine-tuned my newly learned knowledge in sound design and synthesis in general. I taught some classes, traded my Moog for studio time, and performed with several bands; though I was still playing guitar, it was definitely in a diminished role during this time in my life.

I was working at Holze Music in the mid-eighties when the groundbreaking Yamaha DX-7 was introduced. It used frequency modulation (FM) and had a sleek, smooth user interface that left virtually all players scratching their heads. Nothing about it was familiar but it sold like crazy. I sold two to one person, plus a Yamaha electric piano that used real strings. It had just arrived that day and was still in the shipping box. The buyer's purchase condition was that I had to tune it that day because he needed it the following weekend. I took it on because I felt pretty confident in my ear and ability. If memory serves, each note had three strings and the bass register had two each.

"Oh, crap…"

I have the greatest respect for piano tuners now because I was almost in despair over that stupid thing! I had a digital tuner and all the right tools but it seemed impossible to get it right within every interval. I started off by tuning the middle string exactly and then detuning the one on either side slightly sharp and flat to give it the proper motion without sounding like it had a chorus effect on it, the way old saloon uprights sound. Even after I got that right (which wasn't easy), when I started working on octaves, and then fifths, thirds, and fourths, they sounded terrible. They all checked out on the tuner but not against each other. Little did I know at the time that pianos are actually tuned on something called a Railsback curve, meaning that what we perceive as in tune is having the higher notes increasingly sharp and the lower notes increasingly flat the farther they are from middle C. Tune each note on an equal-tempered scale and it sounds horrible. Without going into too much detail, it has to do with the physical properties of the string mass: how long they are, their diameter, etc., because they introduce inharmonicity in the overtones. So the end result is that our perception is more important than being absolutely accurate. Each piano has variations on this curve because of the length of the sound box and other factors. The smaller the box and shorter the strings, the more pronounced the effect. As I say, I didn't know this yet but I had to go with my own ears and that's how I left it. He seemed to be pleased and I vowed never to touch another one.

Technology never sleeps and it has been a dizzying journey through all the advances in recording and sound creation over the years. I've kept up with new gear as interest and finances allowed. I delved into additive synthesis when computers became powerful enough and still marvel at what I learned there. Every sound that exists is made up of sine wave partials or overtones; it's like the atoms of sound — they make up everything. Being able to analyze and see them individually and then tweak them is a sound designer's dream. You can see why Bing Crosby's vocals are so rich and distinct — which partials and formants are prominent and how they vary over time. All the same partials are present and with the exact same intervals, no matter what the sound is; it's just a matter of how loud each one is along with their respective envelopes or volumes, and how inharmonic elements are integrated overall (noise that has no pitch).

My love of music never left me even though I pursued other interests such as woodworking. I would move to Maine and then Colorado before I started composing and performing with any intentionality. But first, I would like to take you back to another landmark moment during my teen years that would forever change me.

Chapter 12

Resonant Frequencies

A fundamental law of physics is that every object has what is called a resonant frequency. That means that every form of matter will vibrate at a certain frequency of sound energy. If you placed a sine wave generator (Come on, don't you have one in your basement?) in your home and played it so that it began below the threshold of hearing and slowly swept it up in pitch until you could no longer hear it (roughly 20Hz-20kHz), and if you played it loud enough, you would hear every object in your home buzz and vibrate at a certain point. Remember Ella Fitzgerald singing and breaking her wine glass in those old commercials? Same principle. The glass broke because it's rigid and brittle and the vibrations overcame its tensile strength. It's much more complicated than that, but my point in bringing it up is that people get excited by (I hate to say vibrate with) certain writers because they think alike; they have the same resonant frequency, so to speak.

C. S. Lewis was on the same frequency as I am. Everything he says makes sense to me and excites me. I know a lot of people say they have a hard time understanding what he's talking about, but that doesn't mean they are less intelligent than I am; it just means that I happen to think along the same lines as he did, so his concepts and illustrations make sense to me immediately. It might be the other way around with a different author. I might be forever lost and you would be singing their praises and genius while doing your valiant best to enlighten me.

Divorce Is Good

I don't know what brought my attention to this particular book by Lewis, but I remember very clearly that I was reading *The Great Divorce* in my backyard on a sunny morning when I was seventeen. I had never read anything else like it before. I was exposed to a line of reasoning and articulate expression that seemed to make me explode inside. I was sitting in a lawn chair with my feet on the ground, but I felt like I was running around the yard yelling, it filled me with so much energy. In his autobiography *Surprised by Joy*, Lewis describes how George MacDonald baptized his imagination while reading *Phantastes*. It felt like Lewis was baptizing my intelligence while I read *Divorce*. My very mode of thought was lifted beyond my ordinary world into something sublime; I couldn't stop reading it and yet I found myself going over whole sections again just to experience that same thrill of discovery.

In my opinion, one of his greatest gifts is his ability to represent both sides of an argument in a fictional setting. Most writers set themselves up to win by how they voice the opposition. Lewis is the opposite: he often paints himself into a corner in such a way that I can't see how he'll get out of it. *The Problem of Pain* is a perfect example. The first two pages are filled with his description of being an atheist and how he would've responded to those who asked him why. The first time I read it, I was shaking my head in disbelief because it was so honest and articulate, and I couldn't see how he would overcome that argument and finally believe in God. One of my pet peeves is that many Christians now forget what it was like to be unbelieving and how they thought and felt at the time they struggled with obstacles of faith. I think that's a huge mistake in relating to other people who are currently stuck at one of those same obstacles.

Another peeve is how few Christians are comfortable sharing their current struggles, as if they suddenly know all the answers and no longer have any questions about certain passages of Scripture or God's role in the world and their lives. What about the Trinity? Even after several thousand years, no one has come up with a comprehensively complete answer. How can three personalities be one and yet totally distinct? How is that different from polytheism if they are all God? Of course, the reason we can't explain it easily is simple: we weren't given all the necessary information to have a complete picture. There may also be another reason: that the very concept and reality is beyond our current mortal ability to understand it. I know the intelligentsia and scientific community don't like to hear something like that, but I think it's a simple matter of humility to admit that it is true. I imagine that even the things we think we do have a grasp of might turn out to have been wrong all along. Or maybe it will be correct, but only as the temporal tip of an eternal iceberg.

Question Everything

Just because I love Lewis doesn't mean I agree with everything he wrote and believed, and I think he would actually be proud of me for critiquing his thoughts. The problem is that he can't fight back now, so I often win my one-sided rebuttal. For example, if he were alive today and in possession of the most recent scientific facts, I don't think he would still believe that evolution took place as it is proposed. Just to be clear, "evolution" literally means "change over time," and no one in their right mind would argue against that. I would say rather that God made His creation to be adaptable to its environment and change accordingly.

Just as a skinny farm boy grows muscles in response to bucking bales of hay all summer, or how finches on the Galapagos Islands had a specific beak size relative to their local food source on each island that other varieties didn't, shows adaptation happens all the time. But to say that a fish somehow analyzed his surroundings (without being able to see himself from above to contrast) and created a specialized camouflage system from scratch strikes me as absurd. And if it was random mutation that just happened to get the colors and patterns right and therefore allowed the fish to survive, it wouldn't know it had gotten it right and would continue to mutate and then lose its survivability.

Never Mind

I often hear Discovery or National Geographic programs talk about how Nature did this or that to some species to accomplish a specific purpose, and I always want to ask, where is the mind of Nature? This is an extremely vague statement for anyone to say from a scientific standard of precision. Exactly where is this CPU and decision making mechanism located? Seems a perfect time to quote the timeless wisdom of Mr. Weasley: "Never trust anything that can think for itself if you can't see where it keeps its brain" (Rowling, *Chamber of Secrets*, 262).

I think the supporters of evolution often borrow purpose and design from the concept of God and creation. If evolution were really true in its purest form, it wouldn't care if any species survived or not, including us. And yet we see the clear desire to fight and survive in us and in every animal species. And what use does evolution have for beauty and wonder — and music? There's no reason or explanation for us to even be aware of the concept of beauty in the first place, because it offers no practical use whatsoever, even as a tool for survival. It's strictly bonus material. But, take those things away and there isn't much of a reason to even want to be alive.

For all the arguments for or against evolution, I don't think there are that many pure intellectuals who honestly seek the truth, and who will follow it no matter where it might lead. Most of us approach this subject with a bias already affecting our judgment and how we process the information available. It's my opinion that no matter how much evidence you examine or how much information you have, you will always be left with a choice to make because no one will ever have all the answers or have been an eyewitness to all historic events. In the end, people believe what they choose to believe.

I've been leading a home church for the last seven years now, which is itself a miracle of sorts if you knew my level of rebellion and history. I'll explain how that even came about in another chapter, but I've always stressed the importance of testing what people say and teach, even if it comes from a favorite, a safe and proven writer or speaker. Don't just accept, part and parcel, what someone's saying (including me). That's also one of the many things I love about C. S. Lewis, that when he eventually acknowledged that God was God, it wasn't for several more years until he was satisfied that Jesus was His Son and our Messiah and Savior. Once Lewis finally believed something, he allowed it to change his behavior, which is incredibly wise and authentic.

Anticipation

It's a very unfortunate thing when you find someone whose writing you love so much, and who is no longer living, because you eventually have nothing else to look forward to. The same thing happened when I fell in love with Led Zeppelin. Everything had already been released and the only album I could anticipate was *In Through the Out Door*, which was very subpar in my opinion. Still, from my early introduction to Lewis, I had a lot of incredible material to explore and challenge my way of thinking. I love re-reading books because I get to again experience my favorite scenes and encounters, in the case of fiction, and word craft and wisdom in the case of nonfiction — and I have read many of Lewis' books over and over. In contrast, my wife Laura usually only reads a book once and then moves on. The exception to this rule was the Harry Potter series and *The Shack*. In the case of the latter, she finished it and turned around and read it again...twice! The other benefit to reading a book more than once is that you often see or understand things differently, depending on your experiences since the last time. This can often provide great contrast, or even resemble triangulation in the sense of looking at the same object but from different perspectives.

As you start gaining confidence in an area of your life, it tends to gather speed and you can build on it from there. For me, that process really began in earnest from this point on. My grandmother might be likened to Paul; my mother to Peter (who was her favorite apostle), though she never chopped off anyone's ear to my knowledge. I guess I've always thought of myself as closer to Stephen: without worldly credibility or formal education, but transformed through my relationship with Christ. Once you become comfortable with who you are, it frees you to explore the world on your own terms instead of everyone else's. Again, there's incredible liberty when Christ lifts you above your boundaries, whether self-imposed or circumstantial.

When Scripture tells us to be conformed into the image of Christ, it's easy for people (including me) to immediately cringe and step back because it sounds like losing our identity and being smooshed in a Play-Doh Fun Factory. That makes me want to run! I don't want to be a star or crescent moon like everyone else. The fantastic news is God doesn't want it either. Take a look at your finger now and remember that your fingerprint is unique among everyone who has ever lived. That's how uniquely you are made. He doesn't want you to be like other people but only to be true to the way He made you to be. The statement to be conformed and yet be unique may sound like a contradiction, but it's not. It's more of a paradox in that the more we yield our lives to Christ, the more we truly become ourselves. It's not some hypothetical idea I'm proposing: I've experienced it firsthand and continue to whenever I'm willing to trust Him. This is because being conformed to the image of Christ sets our eyes on the Author of Life instead of on our self-imposed limits, distorted perceptions, and all the other weights and insecurities that continually hold us back and drag us down. God wants to set us free, and that will only happen when we submit our lives to Him without any reservation.

I Will Choose Freewill

I love the group Rush and have followed them since first hearing their album *2112*. I had it on eight-track (leave me alone!) and I used to turn off the lights in my room and just stare at my stereo display while listening to it over and over. I learned all their songs and eventually read Ayn Rand's book, *Anthem*, on which *2112* was based. I loved Neil Peart's lyrics and intelligent mind, but I couldn't help cringing while listening to their song "Freewill" from the album, *Permanent Waves*:

"You can choose a ready guide in some celestial voice.
If you choose not to decide, you still have made a choice.
You can choose from phantom fears and kindness that can kill.
I will choose a path that's clear, I will choose freewill."

That's so beautifully articulated and expressed, but the problem is that it's wrong — at least in this context. No human is free who is still bound by their fallen appetite and nature. To reject God and all outside influences may sound heroic and leave you feeling like you are a totally free agent, but you are not; no one else is either, and claiming it to be true doesn't make it so. What actually happens is that you abandon help from the One who made you and knows you better than you know yourself, and you therefore remain immersed in all your cultural and experiential biases and injuries. Besides, no one can ever honestly claim to be completely free and independent because we are continually bombarded by media, consumerism, and endless propaganda that affects and influences our worldview. Think about this: how bold would you (or Neil) be in that proclamation if there was no one else around to applaud it?

Zero

If you don't believe that God exists and that we are eternal beings, then none of this matters anyway. You die, and then there is nothing. Zero value. I often hear atheists explain that their life has meaning because they contribute in some way to the assurance that future generations are basically healthy, wealthy, and wise, and that our species somehow continues forever.

First of all, the basic premise is faulty. If your individual life has a value of zero, then so do theirs, and endless generations don't add value to the equation through mere repetition and replication:

0 x 1,000 equals 0;
0 x 1,000,000,000 equals 0;
0 to any power still equals zero.

Secondly, it doesn't do YOU any good at all — you're gone. Let me ask you a question: would you bother working so hard in college to get a doctorate, if the very next day after graduation, you forgot it all? Would you bother going on a magnificent vacation if you couldn't remember that you even went after you got back? This is basically what happens if you don't believe in a future life after this one. Everything you've learned and experienced is gone and worth nothing. Zero value for your life. Zero value for every life that comes after you, too.

If on the other hand, you do believe in God and that you live forever, but just don't want Him meddling in your affairs ("Don't bother me in this life, God, but I *still* want to go to Heaven!"), then we are being kind of presumptuous and arrogant by thinking that we know better how to live our lives than the One who made everything in this universe. To that attitude, God might say, "Okay, take another good hard look at quantum mechanics and then tell Me that you know more than I do."

His desire to restore us back to what He originally intended us to be before our rebellion is perfect and good, and only He can accomplish it. We trust GPS and radar guidance systems to safely and accurately lead us to our destination when we encounter fog while flying, and we literally can't see anything. Why don't we trust the One who actually made the air that we are flying in to do the same with our hearts and minds?

Chapter 13

Heart and Mind Alive

A year after not dating at all, I met Felicia when I was nineteen and working as produce manager at Tusa's Market near Baylor. I enjoyed my time there but it was a little disturbing to see very well-to-do students coming in along with much poorer African-Americans who lived in that area as well. Fortunately, everybody got along and I made good friends on both sides of that economic scale. Mr. Tusa had asked Billy Haney and me if we would play at a nursing home where his mother was staying. Neither one of us wanted to sing, but Billy had a guitar student, Felicia, who had a beautiful voice, so we asked her to go with us. She was excited to be a part of it. I think we played some ELP, Peter Gabriel, and Pink Floyd on acoustic guitar, and everything went well. Some of the nursing home residents even got up and danced. It really didn't matter what we played, they just appreciated the time and attention.

Shortest Job Ever

Felicia and I stayed in touch for several years, until eventually we began dating. We were both very involved in our own churches at the time and I was able to see the difference it made in a relationship when you were both focused on the

Lord. I had been a salesman at Holze Music for two years when we decided to get married. My mother had passed away in 1984 and so Lee Ann and I inherited our home. We wanted to sell it but there was a lot of major work to be done on an addition my father and grandfather had built. Our neighborhood that was developed in the '50s had been a swamp area and the weight of the addition caused the foundation to sink away from the rest of the house. There really wasn't anything to do with it except to tear the addition down. This brought up a big problem because I wanted to do the work to save us money, but I had very little knowledge about construction at that time. Did I say "very little?" How about "none!" I didn't even know what I would find when I removed the door casing. The truth was that I had just returned from my shortest term of employment ever. A friend invited me to apprentice as a finish carpenter under him. It was only two weeks later when he suggested that I maybe try another line of work. Just like having the power shut off during my first concert, it should have discouraged me from ever trying it again, but for some unknown reason, it had the opposite effect. I had my official tool belt and I was eager to take on this mammoth project.

A Dream Is Born

It was around that same time that a dream came into my mind about someday building my own home. To me, this seemed absolutely impossible because I had no experience working with tools. I remember talking on the phone with a dear friend of mine named Albert. This was the same guy who was riding his motorcycle with me when I laid mine down in Cameron Park. When I told him my dream about building my home, he kind of caught me off-guard when he said, "Why not? You can do it." I think the dream became a goal at that moment, and when I ran across a program on designing and building an energy efficient home, I started thinking about the possibility of going there and taking that course. It was taught by a husband and wife team who lived in Bath, Maine. They gave you a choice between taking a three-week crash course in which you spent eight hours every day in class, or going one night a week for fifteen weeks. I decided if I was going to travel that far away, I might as well enjoy myself and embrace the culture.

Remodeling our home was a major challenge but it was eventually completed and we put it up on the market. Lee Ann decided to move to Amarillo with her fiancé, John, and our grandmother. Felicia and I, after getting married, decided to help them move and then leave for Maine from there. We stayed in Amarillo for two weeks and then loaded up our two compact cars and headed out. We each had ninety degrees of viewing area available because everything we could possibly fit was stuffed into those cars right up to the ceiling. We packed sandwiches for lunch and I'll never forget the feeling I had when we stopped to eat in some barren parking lot out in the middle of nowhere. What was I thinking??!! What on earth were we doing driving all the way across the country when neither one of us had jobs lined up or a place to stay? It really was a moment of panic, but we had made a commitment and I could only hope things would somehow work out. The rest of the drive across the country was fun and adventurous and without mishap. What a beautiful country we lived in! Something was happening inside me that I wasn't fully aware of yet. With the exception of a few vacations, I had basically lived my whole life in Texas and now something was awakening in the deepest part of me.

Moose Alert!

As we drove into Maine, we encountered what the locals called a "dog day" — fog as thick as their delicious New England chowder. There were moose alerts on the radio and we laughed at how alien that sounded. However, hitting a full-grown moose on the highway is no laughing matter. Their legs are so long, a normal-size car will take those legs out and the rest of that twelve-hundred pound body will slide right up your hood and into your face. Fortunately, we didn't see any moose that day, but we also didn't see any of the scenery that I had been anticipating for so long. I don't know how we found lodging that first night, but it was in someone's converted barn with bunk beds and no lights. I got top bunk and could sense the ceiling one foot away from my face even in the pitch black. The weather wasn't any better the next morning as we drove toward Bath. We still didn't have a place to stay, so we found a seaside cottage at Popham Beach State Park and called it a night. Being close enough to hear but not see the Atlantic Ocean was both frustrating and intriguing. You could feel its immensity and presence bearing down on you.

The next morning took our breath away. The fog had burned off during the night and nothing but brilliant blue sky greeted us. It seemed all of nature had awakened and our senses were filled to overflowing with the briny smells and furtive cries of the seagulls celebrating the wide world again. What difference a larger vision makes! We couldn't believe all the beauty that was so near us, and yet unseen for a time.

We drove into Bath and at the very first building we walked into, we came out again with jobs and a place to rent. I look back at that time and I'm astounded at my innocence and naïveté. God, however, saw this whole trip as an opportunity to demonstrate His encompassing provision for us. This new chapter opened up a time of blessing that lasted for several years. The only way I can express it is that He seemed to grant me favor in everyone's eyes. I was hand-painting capes for a local contractor just a little older than myself. This occupation afforded me incredible vistas of the surrounding countryside and I felt like I was in heaven after living so long in the Texas heat. One day, the temperature reached a blistering high of eighty-two degrees and everyone had to quit work and sit in the shade for several hours because it was intolerable to them. I laughed and kept working, absorbing the sparkling air and humidity — as well as a little Benjamin Moore paint — into my skin. I was working alongside a lobsterman who was absurdly entertaining and puzzling. All of us got along great, and though I didn't have much experience in painting, I took to it quickly and became their "cutter." This was before painters used 3M masking tape and they needed someone who could paint a straight line when two different colors intersected. Mark Geiger was the owner, and it seemed like he gave me a raise twice a week. He was a wonderful person to work for and with, and it seemed like anytime I made him laugh, he would turn around and give me another raise. I had never worked for someone so emotive before. I liked it.

The place that we were renting was perfect; it was a small, two-story Cape Cod with dark gray shiplap shingles on the exterior and a sloping ceiling with skylights. We even had a washer and dryer, which was almost unheard of in a rental. It's impossible to fully describe the wonder and transformation that was taking place inside me. This was like living in another country that just happened to speak English. It was a completely alien world from what I had grown up in, but it triggered — by its sheer contrast and diversity — all my senses to start recording again, just as we all experience when we are children and everything is new to us. Bath is a charming New England town of about 8,500. It is a very family-centered community and everyone was very friendly…up to a point! People would greet you on the street, but if you stopped to engage them longer or ask questions, then there was a long period (five minutes) in which they would evaluate you before allowing you in any further. Once you passed that test though, their homes and their lives were yours.

We hadn't brought any furniture with us and our new place was minimally furnished, so I set about making an entertainment center and coffee table with the only tool I owned at that time: a miter saw. This forced me to be creative and I bought 1″ x 4″ white pine boards and arranged them in such a way that I didn't need a table saw or other woodworking equipment — just glue and screws. I had never built anything before, so I was very happy with these modest accomplishments.

Come a mild summer evening, everyone who could move would be out walking whatever they had to offer, be it a dog, a child, or a pet iguana. It didn't matter so long as it could walk. I don't remember seeing a lobster on a leash, but the image is pretty comical. "Come on, Pinchy. Move!" We found a church and started making friends pretty quickly. We also found a great pizza parlor called Cabin Pizza, and that's nearly as important. I would imagine it's pretty common among smaller communities, but people really take you to heart in Maine. We had a great time getting together with our new friends and watching the confused expressions from waitresses when we asked for chicken-fried steak or chili. My boss and coworker still swears to this day that I once tipped my hat to a lady in an elevator and said, "Howdy, Ma'am," and thus gave away my place of origin.

On one flawless autumn day in October, our work was canceled and I suddenly found myself with an unexpected time of freedom. I immediately ordered pizza delivery and sat outside and feasted under a sugar maple in our yard, washing the whole thing down with two frosty Dr Peppers. This was one of those perfect moments that stays with you forever. The colors on that tree in particular were absolutely breathtaking. When you see colors like that all over town, it makes you feel like you're singing inside without words or tune. We bought cheap Huffy bicycles from the local department store and rode around as often as we could just to soak in this glorious atmosphere.

Lee Ann and John flew up there to get married and I performed the ceremony in the colorful Maine woods. They had already gone to the justice of the peace beforehand to make it legal, so it was just a formality, but a very special one! A very great privilege to be asked, and one that I would repeat later when my eldest niece, Erin, and her fiancé, Ryan, asked me to marry them.

Not Always Why You Think

My evening classes were going just fine but it felt somewhat disappointing after all the testimonies I had read about from years past. They showed pictures of students lifting hand-hewn beams and pounding in wooden pegs, none of which happened for us. Apparently, that only happened for the day classes and only when someone happened to be building a timber frame home. I really didn't learn all that much, and though it was the primary reason for our being there, it turned out to be the least significant one. If that's what it took to get me out of my comfort zone and into a whole new world of adventure, I count myself very fortunate and it was worth every penny of the tuition.

Our work started slowing down and it was on one fine evening when they had us over for dinner that Mark told me work had run out and I had better start looking elsewhere for a job. I had just finished my classes and Felicia was starting to feel homesick anyway, so we began making plans to move back to Amarillo. I sold my Toyota Corolla very quickly (any car without rust is a prize possession on the East Coast) and we rented a small U-Haul to take our meager possessions back to Texas behind her Mazda RX-7. At the very last moment, I found out there was more work and we could stay in Bath after all, but we were already in motion and kept to our plans.

Six months after our arrival, we left on a snowy day in February. Taking turns, we drove all the way back home straight through, reaching Amarillo after forty-four hours. It fell on my shift to navigate the mountains of Pennsylvania overnight in a powerful snow storm. My jaws were exhausted from clenching my teeth as Felicia slept peacefully next to me. Every time a semi passed us, their airstream would cause us to lose traction and slide sideways. It happened every few minutes and I was exhausted by the time I handed the reins of that rebellious, traction-less, gas-powered horse back over to her. She told me she had looked over a few times during the night and got freaked out because it looked like I was silently screaming. True. I did that to help me stay awake.

Forever Changed

In six months, Maine changed me forever. It opened my eyes and imagination to the potential of life beyond anything I had experienced or imagined before. That's a priceless lesson when you try to imagine Heaven and another world waiting for us after this life — one that is beyond what we can imagine now. Always back to trust, isn't it?

I have to be honest in saying that I never really prayed specifically about moving to Maine. I prayed about the trip and details, but not about the decision. I guess I was operating on the childlike premise that He gives us the desire in the first place, and it's okay to follow your heart. I do believe in the wisdom of seeking Him first, but that's where I was at back then. I still hold to that original concept, but have since learned through pain and disappointment that our desire isn't necessarily His plan or timing. All that being said, His graciousness and provisional demonstration was revealing an intimacy and expression of our relationship I hadn't known before. And it was continuing…

Chapter 14

Howdy, Ma'am

It wouldn't even be noticed if I greeted someone with "Howdy, Ma'am," now that we were back in the un-lobstered regions of Texas. I still have my doubts as to that account in Maine. I mean, I didn't even have a cowboy hat or boots yet! Never trust a five-foot, four-inch lobsterman who looks like Gregg Allman.

As much as I loved my time in Maine, there was a freedom in being back in the Lone Star State that was refreshing. It's like the countryside suddenly relaxed and spread out. The crickets came out at night to serenade us again and lightning bugs hypnotized us with their lazy aerial maneuvers. Endless radio towers sang their familiar siren songs and winked at me with their red eyes. I was back on familiar ground. The wonderful thing about painting is that you can find a job pretty much anywhere. I quickly found a "large" company consisting of exactly one painter — the owner. He had just landed a job painting a very large church by hand and hired me with toothful enthusiasm. He actually looked quite a bit like Jimmy Carter's beer-brewing brother, Billy. There's a country song there somewhere.

Just a Swingin'

Looks can be deceiving, though, as he was sharp as a carpet tack and a brilliant mathematician. He would spend hours meticulously calculating the most efficient use of a sandpaper square (cost vs. time of use) and once he was satisfied with the results, would turn and ask if I wanted to go get some donuts. Talk about the efficient use of time! Three hours later we would head back and continue working. This church was huge and had an even "huger" (sharp as a tack) steeple on top of it. We had to use a forty-foot ladder to get on top of the roof and then another forty-footer to get up on the steeple. There was nothing to stand on at the top so we had to improvise a rope and plank system, in which I would sit suspended for hours each day while re-glazing and painting the seemingly endless mullioned window squares. By the time we finished that steeple, I was deeply tanned since I worked in just a pair of shorts. You could see that church from all around town and the *Amarillo Globe-News* took some great pictures of me swinging seventy feet in the air.

Once we were done, we had to untie the top ladder and then climb down. We were about twenty feet above the roof, when a sudden gust took hold of the ladder and dislodged it from the steeple. I climbed down quickly but my boss had to slide down the remainder — and only just in time! This ladder was heavy duty and fully extended as it came crashing down on the slate tile roof. It scored a perfect diagonal line across those tiles and he had to replace a lot of them. It felt so good to be back near the ground again as we concentrated on the more manageable walls. The church was in a beautiful suburban neighborhood and it wasn't unusual to see people out walking.

There was, however, one young woman who seemed to come by every day, pushing a stroller. I would say "Hi" from my ladder and then return to my work. Eventually, she would come by when I was closer to the ground and we began to talk more. Do you see where this is going? We got to know a lot about each other and our respective families and decided it would be fun for the four of us to get together. Something was subtly troubling to me and I realized I was becoming attracted to her. I thought about this for several days and wondered if I should break our plans. It's funny because there's a pattern that has happened to me over and over that I can no longer discount. This may sound strange, but I think the Lord uses minor pain sometimes to get my attention. On this fateful day, I had decided that I would tell her about my attraction and that it would probably be better not to get together. I was carrying some paint down concrete steps to the basement when I made my decision to go ahead and tell her. At that exact moment I slipped and fell on my butt with the open cans of paint held out at arms' length. My momentum carried me downward and I bounced on each step like a human slinky. I didn't spill a single drop of paint and I wasn't hurt, but I was pretty shaken up. I remember wondering at that moment if it was an "intervention" to stop me from telling the woman about my attraction. I absolutely believe it was now because of the resulting consequences. Electricians will tell you that you're safe as long as the circuit is not completed. I completed it.

Just a Talkin'

By telling her about my attraction, she opened up and told me about hers toward me. She admitted that she walked around the church every day so she could see me up on the ladder. Every one of us likes to know that we are attractive to the opposite sex, and I was no different back then. She was very pretty and it was an ego boost to know that she was attracted to me. It probably happens countless times for everyone, but it only becomes dangerous when it's made known. In this case, "what you don't know won't hurt you" is true. She seemed okay with my decision and I felt good about changing our plans. That night, I told Felicia everything that had happened, all the while still feeling good and responsible about recognizing a dangerous situation and circumventing it. She didn't share the same relief. It wounded her deeply that I would even find another woman attractive at all. We wrestled with it for many days and nights, with me having to recount all the details and timeline over and over until we were both exhausted emotionally. I thought I had done the right thing by bringing it out and telling her. She obviously didn't feel that way at all and it fractured our marriage foundation. We got beyond it but I don't think it was ever the same after that. There was now a new insecurity in her mind that I don't think ever truly left her. If I were to give advise in a similar situation now, I'm not sure that I can say with absolute conviction that there is a right answer. It's probably best to say it depends on the relationship and the personalities involved. As long as the danger is over, it might be better to just let it go without broadcasting it. Not everything needs to be made known. Sometimes it can even be a selfish motive that prompts you to clear the air for your own sake at the expense of someone else's heart. As I think about different couples I currently know, I can see wisdom in both answers. To speak, or not to speak? Regardless, my boss required me to wear a shirt from then on as we finished up the church after six months of painting. We then moved on to other projects and neighborhoods so there was no more awkwardness from working close to the "other woman."

We had moved back in with Lee Ann and her husband, John, so there were five of us living together, including my grandmother. We all got along very well and spent a lot of time together. I had always wanted to live in Colorado, and still being young and adventurous, we talked about the many different possibilities available to us now. It soon became a dangerous thing for us to visit a place because we might end up moving there, often overnight. My sister was still carrying around four bedrooms' worth of furniture and items that she felt sentimental about after losing our mother to cancer. Not even in an alternate universe could all that be packed into a Mazda RX-7. The days of traveling relatively light were quickly coming to an end as we all — Felicia and I, and Lee Ann and John — rented a large moving van and packed everything up to move to Colorado Springs and Security, respectively. Lee Ann and John were both nurses and could find a job almost anywhere. This time I ended up working for a company that had one hundred painters. They did a lot of industrial work and sprayed everything. I didn't really care for this job experience, especially when they put me in an interior building using industrial epoxy without a respirator. I had a tremendous headache that first night and refused to go back to that same task the next day, so they put me on a motorized scaffold and I raced around a new mall parking lot, painting light poles. This was fun, if a little unnerving! When you hit the gas four levels up, there's a delay before you start moving as the tower sways. Same with braking, apparently. They sent a few of us up to Vail for two weeks to paint a new hotel and that was a blast. When we got back I was informed by a friend that they would be laying people off soon and I was on the short list since I was a new hire.

Just a Movin'

We had moved into a townhouse on a hill and had a great view of Colorado Springs. The only problem was moving my studio piano up three flights of stairs. Thankfully, the "incredible hulk" lived nearby and he basically carried it all the way up, lifting the heavy lower end by himself. My grandmother was living with Lee Ann and John in Security, but we would have her over periodically to stay the night. One morning Felicia and I were sitting in the living room and my grandmother came out of her bedroom carrying a Maxwell House coffee can. We both knew what was in it — pee. Because she was crippled and couldn't easily walk to the bathroom, she would just go in the can if the need arose during the night. Maxwell's famous slogan was therefore altered to "Good until the last drop." So we sat and watched her scoot on her knees while carrying this dangerous cargo up to the island counter. She then lifted it up over her head and unceremoniously dumped the whole can into the sink which held all our dishes from the previous night. Such is life, and why dishwashers were invented.

Felicia had been held up at gunpoint at her job at Safeway and I wasn't thrilled with my employment anyway, so once again we began looking at the atlas for our next move after only four months. Down the piano went again, but without "Mr. Muscle" this time. There were several places that sounded good: Winter Park, Evergreen, Woodland Park, etc. I didn't know anything about them, but I liked the names. Estes

Park looked good because it bordered Rocky Mountain National Park and I wanted snow! Everywhere I moved I thought I'd finally get some in quantity, but I kept hearing the same thing: "Oh no, we get some snow, but they get *tons* of it just twenty miles from here!" I'd heard the same thing in Bath and now here in Colorado, too. Surely this place called Estes Park would get lots of snow; after all, they were right next to the Continental Divide.

Chapter 15

Estes Park

One weekend in 1988, the four of us decided to go up to Estes Park and have a look around. We loved what we saw and stayed all night, landing jobs the next day. Back we went to load up another moving van (and grandmother) and we all moved to Estes. We rented a house together on Graves Avenue, but after only a month, John and Lee Ann had to move back to Texas to care for his grandparents. Felicia and I had to move into a very small guest cabin behind the main house because it was too expensive by ourselves. This was tiny by anyone's standards, but it was fairly comfortable. We ended up moving several times to nearby locations for one reason or another over the next couple of years. Grandmother was staying with us at this point and that was always an adventure. One evening we were all sitting in front of the television and I was trying to switch channels quickly in case we ran across Lawrence Welk, because Grace might see it and then we would be destined for an hour of mind-numbing "entertainment." All of a sudden, Felicia jumped up in front of us and started dancing and removing her robe, eventually standing there before us completely naked. Grandmother just started laughing hysterically. Felicia had felt a spider crawling on her and panicked. Well, this new, unexpected form of entertainment certainly took everybody's mind off Mr. Welk!

When Lee Ann and John moved back a year later, we rented a house together on Mall Road right by Lake Estes. The views were incredible and I bought a new rod and reel and fished almost every day after work. This new location also provided another unbelievable opportunity. For the last couple of years, we had to face the maniacal crowds to watch the Fourth of July fireworks and then try to get back home, which often took an hour to go only a few blocks. Now we merely sat our chairs out on our property and enjoyed the fireworks shooting off right over our heads — and without anyone around us. This was incredible! And as the smoke and final echoes faded away, we turned our chairs around to watch all the red brake lights lining up for miles trying to get out of town. This was almost as entertaining as the show itself.

Cat Tails

My sister had a cat named Murgatroid and it deeply affected his brain. He would rub up against your leg until you finally reached down to pet him and then you would come back up with a bloody stump. Very crazed and unpredictable, but she loved him and so he remained in the land of the living. One day, John and I were alone with the beast when he came streaking through the living room like a black comet. The living room had a door at each end that connected to the kitchen on the other side of the wall so he could complete his eccentric orbit with regularity. A few seconds later, he reappeared with frantic purpose, as if the fairies were pulling sparks from his tail. What the hell was wrong with him now? Was this just another trick so we would compassionately reach out to him and be decapitated for our troubles? The next circuit give us a glimpse of some object that was attached to his hindquarters and so we paid particular attention on the next round. He even stopped momentarily to bite at it before taking off again so we could have a better glimpse. It looked like an eight-inch string was stuck to him, so we both started trying to step on it as he ran by each time. I was barefoot and happened to get the timing right and immediately wished I hadn't. The string was not stuck to his behind at all, but was issuing fourth from said orifice. He had swallowed a three-foot string and had only passed that much of it. The smell that rose up to greet us was indescribable. I would also imagine the novel experience of having his entire intestinal passage instantly flossed by the remaining two feet of string was entirely indescribable as well. He just sat there staring off into space in the afterglow.

It was a hate-hate relationship but we seemed to entertain each other at least. I would try to thump his ears and he would make me bleed for it. One other pay-per-view event happened in that house when I was alone with him. There was a closet door that led down into the crawl space through a plywood trap door. It had a three-quarter-inch hole drilled into it so you could put your fingers in to lift it, and then walk down the stairs. Someone forgot to close the door and "Murg" stuck one of his paws through to investigate. As soon as I walked by and saw him, he instantly swelled and then couldn't withdraw his paw. He panicked even more as he realized his predicament and began hopping around in a circle like a three-legged rabbit trying to pull his paw out. I tried to keep my opportunistic thoughts and fantasies from his cat mind and console him, but he wouldn't listen to reason; so I had to simply leave him alone until he shrank again to normal proportions. He later walked by and looked at me with cool insolence as if nothing had ever happened.

The last noteworthy occurrence happened when he jumped up on the windowsill right behind the couch I was sitting on, just looking for trouble. Previous wounds hadn't healed yet so I partially donned a ski glove for protection and started rapidly poking at him while he frantically swatted at me. The transcendent moment came when the glove accidentally flew off my hand, got wedged behind the couch, and just happened to pin his neck against the window. He stopped moving and just screamed. I couldn't get him to stop, even when I backed away so he could see that my hands were nowhere near the glove. Maybe he thought I was throttling him by remote control. It was one of the few moments that I truly felt sorry for him and his inability to make a simple connection.

Calling My Bluff

I had been painting in Estes for three months when again, the work ran out. We were talking to my former boss, Mark, in Maine and he offered me a foreman position with a big increase in pay. We were within a couple of days of heading back northeast when Felicia told me about a job that had just opened up at the YMCA where she worked. It was the cabinet maker position and I thought that would be ridiculous since my furniture repertoire consisted of exactly one stereo cabinet and one coffee table. But I thought, "What the heck," and put in my application...I got the job.

November 15, 1988, I became a cabinet maker. I couldn't believe it! What was I going to do now? The next morning I was standing in the woodshop waiting for my orientation and peeking into everything that was around, trying to figure out how it was assembled. My new boss looked like Lucas McCain on *The Rifleman*. He was, in fact, a former Green Beret and scared the hell out of me. He eventually called me into his office and gave me my first project: twelve simple outdoor benches, and I breathed a sigh of relief. I could handle this, and thus I began my first steps toward confidence, knowledge and security in my new position. Lee Sanderson was built like a tank, but he was actually very gentle and easy to work with. His son, Dwayne, might not give the exact same reference, but I soon gained a lot of respect and comfort working for Lee. Every time I finished one project, I feared what would come next. When would I be discovered as a fraud and tossed out? I always managed to stay just ahead of what I needed to know and do, and after a couple of weeks, I finally started to relax a little and believe I could do this. Remember when portable CD players had to buffer a few seconds ahead so they could play uninterrupted? That was me — ahead in my knowledge by just a few hours. Years later, when my next supervisor Jon Landkamer and I had been good friends long enough, he told me I was hard to give advice to back then. I didn't realize that until he said it, but I had to laugh because I knew it was true — and instantly knew why: I was insecure about my position. I thought I should know everything already and was afraid to admit that I didn't because I might lose my job. The freedom to trust people and allow them to walk beside me and tackle something together wouldn't come until later.

The way everything was set up, it couldn't have been more perfect for me and my temperament. Managers often use football positions as an analogy for their work force. I always thought of myself as a wide receiver — part of the team and yet separate and distinct. The woodshop was an unattached building near the main buildings and grounds structure. Again separate, but part of the team. By now, I knew pretty well how I worked best: give me space and tell me what you want done and I'll figure out how to do it. It really was perfect because after determining that I was proficient and that my work ethics were top-notch, they just left me completely alone. When I was finished with one project, they would give me the next one. I remember the elation I felt when I had gone full circle and started on projects I had already done before. My confidence and comfort really grew leaps and bounds from that point on and I thought I had the best job in the world.

Felicia and I got involved in a local church and made lots of friends in town and at the Y. There was aways something fun going on when surrounded by so many people our own age. That December, we went to the Y Christmas party. We didn't see anyone we knew and sat at a table by ourselves. A few minutes later, a couple walked up and asked if they could sit with us. Ole and Katy Sykes joined us and we began a friendship that would grow and deepen over the years. They are still some of my closest friends today. Felicia and I were having fun, but there was still some hurt from the event in Amarillo, as well as other underlying issues that we hadn't dealt with.

The Unmentionable Word

Felicia had never had the chance to be on her own. She had lived with her father and grandmother, and then went into our marriage with its responsibilities, without exploring life as a young single woman. This started to really bother her, as well as her own rebellion toward the church and its moral expectations. I won't say what I felt were her issues but I know that one of mine was communication, or the lack thereof. We talked all the time and laughed a lot, but when she was doing something that bothered me, I failed to tell her. This attitude is so unhealthy and it allows small resentments to build, and then they spill out – often all at once — which is pretty overwhelming if you've ever been the recipient. I was aware that I was withholding those things, but in my mind, it felt like I was being kind and "not making a big deal of it." The problem with that (aside from what I just mentioned) is that it can be a selfish attempt at making yourself a better person instead of giving the other person the same opportunity to better themselves. Does that makes sense? I was only thinking about how I could grow. Now I'm a firm believer in allowing people to just be themselves, but there has to be moderation in all things, as the Lord would teach me very soon.

We knew our marriage was in trouble and went to our pastor for help. There was a godly couple that often counseled people and I was so hoping the wife would be the one assigned to us. We were given her husband instead, and I could only hope it would go well in spite of my misgivings. It was not to be. I sat there absolutely speechless as he personally related to Felicia's rebellion and in subtle ways actually encouraged her to follow her heart and leave. How could he be saying these things when he was a well-known Bible teacher in town? Maybe I sensed even then that she was probably going to leave no matter what was said, and so I never confronted that man of God. I still believe this to be true today. I should also say that I have tremendous respect for that man and don't harbor resentment toward him now. Maybe he was speaking out of his own wisdom and experience and knew Felicia would leave regardless of what he said.

And so on Valentine's Day, 1990, Felicia left. I know for a fact that she didn't choose this day to hurt me; it just happened to be on that day. I can also assure everyone that Valentine's Day didn't become a specialized source of pain forever after — I didn't even think about it when it came around over the years. She moved down to Boulder and began making new friends and a new life. We stayed in touch and would talk on the phone often, and though I don't want to talk about the details of her life, it's important for everyone to know that as much as we were both hurting, we still got along great and never fought about our issues or our possessions. In fact, it was about as friendly as it could possibly be, considering that we were now separated and heading toward a divorce. I heard about her new friends and boyfriends when she'd call, and though that was pretty hard at the time, I still felt that our friendship was important and that I needed to be there for her as she made this new transition in life.

My family was completely supportive, of course, and my brother-in-law wept with me on our deck when he saw the pain I was in, and I so appreciated his tenderness. I also went to see Ole and Katy one evening when I was overcome with grief, and they took me into their arms in the most beautiful way and comforted me, which I will also never forget. I won't try to speak for Felicia and everything she was going through, as that's her own story to tell, but having friends and family right there made all the difference in the world. At an earlier point, before Felicia left, my grandmother's age and health required her to have more care than we could provide. We had to admit her into Prospect Park Nursing Home in Estes, which broke our hearts. Since both Lee Ann and John worked graveyard shifts on weekends, they usually stayed down in the valley for several nights, and this left me alone during a very hard time.

Vulnerable

One Saturday night, I was sitting in our darkened living room, looking out at the lake and reflected lights and it was just too much. I felt so lonely and desperate that I did something I have never done before in my life. I decided to drive down and go to a bar in Boulder with the intention of picking someone up and bringing them back up with me. It's funny that when you know you're doing something stupid, you tend to drive or move faster, as if you can stay just ahead of your conscience and good sense. I made it down and parked in a neighborhood just behind a bar. I got out of my truck and was hit with a pain in my abdomen that stopped me in my tracks. It only lasted a few seconds, then I started walking and it hit me again. I immediately thought about those concrete steps in Amarillo and the lesson I learned then, wondering if the same thing was happening. Dismissing it (because I wanted to), I began walking toward the bar a third time when the pain dropped me to my knees right there in the street. This time I actually laughed out loud and said, "Okay! I give up!" I turned around and got in my truck and began my unaccompanied journey back up to my incredibly romantic and empty home on the lake.

I'm sure there are those who will dismiss the notion of divine protection, but there is absolutely no doubt in my mind that that's exactly what it was. If I had spiritual eyes at that moment, I probably would have seen an angel with a sword physically preventing me from entering that bar on that desperate night. I've done other stupid things without intervention, so why this time? Only God knows what might have happened if I had followed that path and what He actually protected me from. I know He always protects His own because of His encompassing love, but I can't help but think about that night long ago when my grandmother made some sort of covenant with the Lord. One day, I'll know the answer.

I don't remember what I did when I got home; it might have been reading a book for a while and then going to sleep. It certainly wasn't anything romantic or fulfilling. Sometimes, you just have to suck it up and bleed inside.

Chapter 16

Cabin in the Woods

One month before Felicia and I split up, I had put a down payment on two acres of land in Allenspark, a small community sixteen miles south of Estes Park and one thousand feet higher in elevation. This was a partial realization of that dream that had taken root back in the early '80s, so there was no way I was going to let it go without a fight. I was thirty years old and separated, which was hard enough to deal with, but at least I could hold on to that dream even though there was no way that I could imagine ever doing anything with it. The problem was money. Even though our settlement was completely peaceable, it hurt both of us financially to be without the other's income. We had bought a new 4x4 Mazda truck in Maine and I wanted to hold on to that because I was living high in the mountains and needed it. Felicia was fine with letting it go because she was going to be down in Boulder and so she bought a car. But having both a new truck payment and a property payment, as well as some other surviving debt, was going to take me underwater. No one outside of a management position will ever get rich working at the YMCA. I had to take a fifty percent cut in pay from what I had been making in Maine to take that cabinet maker position. I still felt so blessed to have that job, but I wasn't making enough to cover all my expenses, so I had to come up with a solution quickly.

The Good Life

I even thought about living in a tent if I had to — anything to hold on to those two acres. However, living in a tent at 8,500-foot elevation during the winter didn't seem very smart. That's when I drove around the Y property and came across a cabin that looked like it was privately owned. I inquired and found out that some property on the grounds was grandfathered in and still remained private. I found the number to the landlord and asked him about renting it. He said it was available and that I could stay there for $100 a month, plus $8 for utilities. That meant electricity year-round and water for two months in the summer. Four walls and a roof looked a whole lot better than tent fabric, so I took it! I had less than one month to figure out how to survive in this tiny place without heat. Remember, only two years before, this man had been blistering in the Texas heat! It was more than a little intimidating to me to think about living in this 10' x 20' cabin. Anywhere else in the country, this would be called a shack, but in the mountains it's called "rustic". Pretty funny how geography dictates the descriptive title.

I found an old Franklin wood stove and asked my new landlord if I could install it. He gave me permission and so I put it in and then made a trip to Loveland to buy a Stihl chainsaw so I could gather firewood quickly. This set me back about $450, but it was one of the best investments I could've made since I'm still using it to gather firewood twenty-three years later. I got permission from my supervisor to cut down dead-stand aspen on the Y property. It was already fall and the nights were getting cold and crisp, which made me both excited and a little apprehensive. Every day after work and on weekends, I would go out into the woods and fell trees, hauling the rounds back up to my little cabin to hand-split later. Fortunately, aspen is one of the easiest woods to split by hand, but it was still a lot of hard work trying to get ready before the first snow came.

By chance, I happened to meet someone who had lived in that very same cabin years before. He casually informed me that I would have to store all my foodstuffs in the warmest place in the cabin so it wouldn't freeze. I said confidently that place must be by the wood stove I had just installed. He slowly shook his head with a disturbingly knowing look and responded, "In the refrigerator." I stared back at him, uncomprehending. And then it slowly dawned on me: I would only be there for several hours in the evening with the wood stove going. All the rest of the time, the cabin would be a few degrees above the outside temperature. This concept really freaked me out! The refrigerator would be the warmest place in the cabin. Lordy, Lord! How was I going to survive this experience? And so I dutifully stored everything in there, including vegetable oil and other items I never thought about before — anything that shouldn't freeze.

Introspection

Even though this was potentially a pretty depressing time, there was a change that was beginning to work its way through me. I was now very confident in my woodworking skills and I was beginning to find strength in my new lumberjack career as well. I gathered as much as I thought I would need and settled in for my first winter. I didn't have water or phone service, but I had plenty of books to read and music to listen to. It was scary, but it was also a great distraction to keep my mind occupied and off the fact that I was single and heading toward a divorce. I knew the minor complaints I had about Felicia and how they contributed to our marital problems, but in this small quiet cabin, I had to make the choice about looking at myself honestly, and what I needed to change. For the first time since feeling hopeless when I was twelve, I had to completely open my life up to the Lord again and ask Him to reveal those things that I needed to change. In the same way as before, He was so tender in how He brought things to my attention that I couldn't have been aware of otherwise. My communication skills were one of the first things I had to confront. I saw that it was far better and far healthier to let people know how you were feeling and release any pressure before it built up. Geologists are comforted as long as they see Mount Saint Helens venting, because they know there's no danger. When it's quiet and there's nothing coming out, that's when they start paying close attention, knowing it's only a matter of time before a catastrophic explosion will happen.

It's so important to put something like this into practice and not just keep it as an intellectual exercise or simple acknowledgment. Truth needs to take a visible form of expression or it has no purpose. Even light itself doesn't seem real to us until it shines on an object and illuminates it. Think about a laser beam shining in the dark right in front of you; you wouldn't even be aware of it without smoke or dust particles or some particulate matter to reveal its presence. So when the first opportunity came through some misunderstanding with a coworker, I became purposeful in seeking that person out to talk it through. The results were so encouraging that it became easier each time to make the effort. Pretty soon, it felt intolerable if I couldn't contact someone involved in a problem that same day. Wow, what a change already from how I had grown up!

Liberty

The next major upheaval in my perspective and habits came through working in my woodshop. I realized that I had always been liquid in the sense that I accommodatingly flowed around people and objects, much like a river flows around rocks. It never occurred to me that I could move the rocks and flow where they had been! This truth about myself was revealed to me as my confidence and knowledge grew and I realized the former cabinet maker in that woodshop had positioned all the machines according to what made sense to him. It's hard to convey the epiphany I felt when I realized I had the authority to change everything around to suit my own needs. I was the cabinet maker now and I could do whatever I wanted with the shop that was entrusted to me. I felt the way you would if you had lived in someone else's home for several years and then bought it. Those ugly curtains? Down they go! The orange Formica counter that makes you want to sing the theme to *The Brady Bunch*? In the fire! Then, you start to realize that it's not just limited to the hideous; it also means you can tear down a wall because it would be much more efficient to be able to walk through that barrier. Oh, the freedom! It felt so incredible to start moving everything around according to my own personalized workflow, and it made everything so much more efficient. From that stage, I started building jigs for assembly and changing furniture designs to help withstand the continual abuse they suffered.

Again I say: anytime Christ intervenes in your life, the purpose is to liberate you from limited perspective or harmful habits that you carry around for various reasons. I simply can't stress this enough. As C. S. Lewis said, "The universe rings true, wherever you fairly test it" (Lewis, *Joy, 262*). This isn't some hypothetical conjecture I speak of. It is from my own personal experience — fairly tested and true.

I Say Goodbye to Church

I need to step back in time here, and talk about something that happened immediately after our counseling came to an end and Felicia left. The pastor of our church called me into his office and informed me that I was no longer free to date or remarry. Even though I was still too accommodating at that time, there was no accommodation in me at that moment. When he finished speaking, I informed him that though I respected his authority and knowledge, I didn't agree with him at all. I would remarry if the Lord saw fit to bring the right woman into my life. My low-level rebellion against religion quickly rose to the top and I walked away from church fellowship. I did not walk away from my relationship to the Lord, but I did remove myself unwittingly from the protective and encouraging aspect of being around other believers. That particular church at that time also struck me as cliquish and resembling a country club more than what I thought a church should be. That opened up an extra weekend day and began a pattern that I would carry for many years: hiking with friends on Saturday and then holing up in my cabin on Sunday. This was the best of both worlds to me because I love both solitude and social time. All these experiences, even my rebellious ones, were reforming and shaping my character into something which would find a healthier form of expression later.

I was starting to feel sure that I wouldn't freeze to death in that cabin, but there were some humorous moments. I found a large metal bucket that I could fill with snow and then melt on the stove to serve as a humidifier. One morning, I was starting a fire and happened to look over at the bucket that was sitting beside it. I saw two tiny ears and beady black eyes staring back at me. The water had frozen solid during the frigid night and trapped a mouse with his head just above the water line. It's always a little disconcerting when you find life (or former life) staring at you. Maybe he was soaking in the shiny hot tub after I went to bed and the water was still medicinally hot, humming his mousy tunes and keeping an eye on me when the inevitable cold returned and claimed him.

Moonlight Skiing

If I didn't have other plans, I would come to my cabin after work, start a fire, and then take my new cross-country skis up into the park and ski in the moonlight while the cabin warmed up to tolerable levels. It was hauntingly beautiful up there, but if the wind was blowing (ninety percent of the time it was), then I would often find myself turning around quickly, thinking that I heard a pack of coyotes stalking me from behind. I really began to relish my living situation, and though it was often a hardship, like having to use the outhouse located twenty feet away from my cabin, I began to find my rhythm in that unique accommodation and let the peace and stripped-down lifestyle begin to heal me on the inside.

Sometimes I would come back from my midnight tour and find the cabin had grown too uncomfortably hot, and I would have to leave the door open a little bit when I went to sleep, always hoping I wouldn't wake up in the middle of the night to find an animal gnawing on me. One evening, I opened the front door to go to the bathroom and the landlord's crazed golden retriever came crashing into me at a full run. It's as if he knew exactly when I would open that door and timed it perfectly. Another strange and funny encounter with that dog came as I was trying to push his owner's truck out of a snow bank with him nipping and snapping at the back of my legs. Strange pair, those two.

The outhouse was a curious affair, consisting of two sheets of 3/4" plywood attached at the top to form an A-frame structure. The funny thing was that it had a Dutch door, where the top and bottom halves open separately, so you could look out at the road and wave at anyone passing by. Now gather 'round, children, and I shall tell you a tale! One that will fill you with horrific wonder and increase your appreciation for running water exponentially.

It's 7 a.m.: Do You Know Where Your Underwear Is?

By now, you should all know that I love pizza. If you don't, then you're not paying attention. One fine summer evening, I had a pizza and one or two Dr Peppers. Delicious. The next morning, I finished off the leftovers and washed it down with another Dr Pepper. Apparently this was too much carbonation combined with spicy pepperoni and sausage for my system to handle. My stomach started churning like Mount Vesuvius having a tantrum. I instantly knew I had seconds to spare before the inevitable happened. I ran out the door without even closing it and launched myself into that A-framed bomb shelter. I quickly yanked down my shorts just in time before the moment of reckoning came. As I sat there, I experienced what people call a warm and fuzzy feeling. I suspect they mean something entirely different from what I was experiencing. I looked down and realized that my "yank" hadn't included my underwear along with my shorts. I can't even begin to describe the emotions that rolled over me, especially when I remembered that the water had not been turned on yet. I think that's enough detail for now until you're all a little bit older.

My grandmother understandably liked a change of scenery every once in a while, and began imploring me to bring her to my cabin for the night. I tried to explain my primitive living conditions, but she was of a hearty generation and couldn't be deterred. So I picked her up and brought her home for a complimentary summer night at the "Mountain Château." This was a one-bedroom suite so we had to share our slumber on the same full-sized mattress. Neither one of us had any problem with that arrangement, but at some predestined moment in space/time, and in the still of the night when there was no sound or movement except possibly the hot tub mice, my grandmother burst forth in unattenuated volume, "I HAVE TO PEE!" I nearly left my skin behind. I was already awake and there was no warning from the sound of her mouth opening, nor was there a normal person's ramping up on the first couple of words. It was just a pure rending of the night and of my nerves. Only one other time have I had that experience, and that was in the cabin right across the road, when a pack of mischievous adolescent coyotes broke out into their full-volume yips and yaps right next to me. My heart wasn't made for these extremes.

Chapter 17

Choose Life

It wasn't all fun and games in this cabin as I looked down the vanishing point of my life and saw only arid desert in front of me without any hint of change or improvement. I was able to hold on to my two acres of dream, but every two weeks I was left with only thirty-five dollars after bills, and out of that remainder had to come gas, groceries and anything else I needed. Simple luxuries like entertainment and pizza were only seen from afar. Once, after careful consideration, I decided to "invest" eighteen dollars for a subscription to *Astronomy* magazine for one year. At least this would give me something to look forward to every month.

When everything is stripped away, you begin to understand how little we really need to be happy. There were times when I came back from a trip to Denver and I would experience the sharp contrast in altitude and culture and how married they were to each other. From a bustling metro lifestyle, I came up the canyon and through Estes Park resort living, then past the Y community I knew so well. Up, up into the clouds and finally onto an unplowed dirt road as far as my truck would take me before getting stuck in the snow drifts, finally postholing the final distance to my cabin. I didn't need to worry about parking in the middle of the road and blocking it because there wasn't anything beyond that point except God. It really felt like the end of the world to me when I made that journey, especially at night.

Spring Eternal

I was finally able to pay off some bills and that allowed my world to open up considerably. I had made it through my first winter and new staff started arriving for the spring and summer season. Every year, more than 400 young people from around the world came to work at the Y. The potential for new friendships and adventure thrilled me, but I began to recognize that most of them were of college age, somewhere between eighteen and twenty-three on average. I got to meet a lot of them during my workday and at lunch, but I began to feel a little self-conscious about being ten years older than most of them — and separated. I was feeling lonely after the solitude of winter, but I was also shy and unsure about trying to enter their world. Every afternoon and evening from May through September, it felt like being at a carnival. Everyone who was done with their work shift gathered outside to play volleyball or tennis, sit on the porch and play guitar, or just gather around in small circles to talk and laugh. I desperately wanted to be a part of that. I finally made a very hard decision to take the risk and started going down every day to just hang out and see what happened. Everyone was extremely warm and receptive and I quickly found my feet and lost my self-consciousness. It was absolutely wonderful and invigorating, partly because it was absolutely fluid; there were no expectations or structure and therefore plans and activities happened naturally and spontaneously. Friday and Saturday nights always carried the pressure of having a date where I came from. Here, there was none of that at all, and it was so incredibly refreshing! People gathered in groups of two, or five, or twenty-five, and no one thought anything about it.

I was coming to life again and this unique atmosphere allowed me to develop friendships and just have fun without any complications or expectations to dampen it. Going into town alone with a woman? No problem. I've never experienced another place and condition like it anywhere else. I was able to buy some hiking equipment and every weekend provided opportunities to explore the National Park with different people each time. I even started leading groups of people through a cave system known as Old Man Mountain. Every day was a new adventure and I was loving life again when I started to notice something very disturbing. Many of my new friends who were women started treating me differently. All the warmth was gone, and I felt like they were always trying to get away from me now. I had absolutely no interest in trying to pursue a relationship with any of them — yes, because I was still legally married, but more importantly, because I wasn't emotionally ready yet. I still had a lot of healing and processing to do and was totally content and happy with just being friends. So, what was going on??

A Thorn in My Side

There was a woman who knew Felicia when she worked at the Y who was a vicious gossip. When Felicia left because of our separation, she began spreading all kinds of rumors about the reasons why we had broken up — ridiculous things, like how Felicia wanted a baby and I wouldn't give her one. There were probably many other ones just as appalling that I never heard, but the consistent theme was always that I was the bad guy. The height of insult and absurdity came when she actually approached me and asked me out on a date! I couldn't believe that any human was capable of something so contradictory and silly. The "thousand insults of Fortunato" raced through my mind and it was everything I could do not to tell her what I really thought of her and invite her down to the nitre-encrusted catacombs for some brickwork. Maybe I should have, but I can't imagine what the result of that would've been. As it was, she took my rebuff to heart and started going to every woman that she saw me talking to and telling them mean things about me, or at least trying to scare them off with the fact that I was still married and to stay away from me. How vindictive and shallow can a person be? It was some time before I even found out why my new friends were distancing themselves from me, and the resulting awkwardness I felt before I knew their reasons only exacerbated the situation. I would have told those women about my current state of separation from my wife as I got to know them, but I never even got that chance because the gossipmonger preempted that; therefore it only came across as something I was trying to hide.

That troubled woman finally left town but I was still surrounded by the carnage she had created out of spite. It seemed to spread and affect many other young women that I only desired to have a friendship with. The injustice of this hurt my heart so much, but I chose not to retreat from the decision I had made to get involved with the summer staff. I wish my communication skills had been further along by then so I could have sat each one down and articulated everything I was feeling and what the truth really was. I'm sure I stumbled and bumbled my way down that road somewhat, which helped a little bit, but it was still a long and distressing episode when everything else was going so well. God is good though, and at the end of the summer, several of them got together and realized what had happened and invited me to breakfast as an apology and goodwill gesture. I so appreciated their kindness and many of us have since reconnected on Facebook decades later.

Back in the Saddle

Another area of growth happening simultaneously was a decision to take chances and not worry about the results. At the same time I had discovered the freedom to rearrange things in my woodshop, I was finding the freedom to reach out in ways that I wouldn't have before. My new mantra became, "I would rather try and fail than to forever regret not trying at all." This attitude was revolutionary to my inner being. A newly found security and knowledge of my true identity in Christ was setting me free in ways that I couldn't imagine before. I started to truly understand how bound by the fear of rejection we all are in our everyday lives. All of us want to be accepted and liked, and left to our own futile attempts at bolstering our self-worth, we end up making decisions based on how someone else will respond. I became determined to be who I wanted to be without any consideration of how someone else would respond, or if it would be favorable or not. Adopting this attitude was like suddenly discovering that you were really right-handed after using your left hand for many years — or vice versa. The feeling of emotional coordination came quickly, and like all liberating moments, built strength-upon-strength as I exercised this new freedom. I'm sure that some of my more intuitive readers will recognize that the very writing of this book will place me in that extraordinarily vulnerable position once again and test that twenty-year-old resolve.

A very simple example of this was my decision to wave at people from my truck anywhere within a mile of my home and not worry about whether they waved back or not. It may sound silly, but it really helped to establish my actions and work toward making them habitual. I still do this today. Since I was now legally single, it also manifested itself in asking out women whom I never would have before. I knew I would get shot out of the saddle many times, but the whole point of it was that I didn't care any longer; it was more important to not have any regrets. One Saturday morning, I was watching a local newscast out of Denver and noticed the anchor wasn't wearing a wedding ring. Okay, here was an opportunity to test it! I looked up the station number and quickly dialed before I could change my mind. Someone answered and I asked for this anchor and they handed her the phone. Damn! I wasn't expecting this, I just thought they would give me her voicemail. I started laughing and asked, "How do you go about asking someone for a date who's on television?" She started laughing, too, which really put me at ease. The awkwardness and unfairness of it was instantly apparent: I could see her, but she couldn't see me. I suggested that we set up a time for me to come by the station to meet her, so it would be safe, and then we could talk later. My sister, her husband, and I were on our way to the symphony when we stopped by. I told the receptionist that I was there to meet her and waited a couple moments. Out she walked in her business suit and we visited for about fifteen minutes. I think it's the same experience for everyone when they meet a television personality — to be surprised at how short they are. She was very nice and easy to talk to, but there's always an awkwardness when you're standing in a place like that, especially for the purpose of evaluating each other. She seemed to like me and we started talking about when we could go out.

Two things interfered with that happening: her unbelievably busy schedule and my stark awareness about my living conditions. Could I really ask a local celebrity to put on snowshoes to hike up to my cabin after getting stuck in the snowdrifts? One of her closets was probably larger than my whole residence, and what if she had to go to the bathroom? This was just too much. I had proved to myself that I could do it, but there didn't seem any reason to push it into the ridiculous, so I told her one day that in considering the distance between us (in all ways!), it might be better to just let it go.

All in all, it felt incredibly good to do these kinds of things. Sometimes they accepted and sometimes I did get shot out of the saddle, but I was proving that my self-worth didn't depend on the result. Finding that someone misunderstood me was a little bit harder. Walking out of a conversation with someone and knowing that not only did they not know my heart and intention accurately, but would now carry a distorted perception of me based on that misunderstanding, always left me feeling wronged and deeply troubled. As I had just learned recently, it's often better to go right back to that person and clear everything up, but that option isn't always available because of time, accessibility, or the simple conviction that if you tried, you would somehow only dig yourself in deeper because you are on an entirely different wavelength. Again, sometimes you just have to walk away bleeding a little bit inside.

Who's Your Daddy?

Now, this is what makes situations like that tolerable. When you know that the Creator of the universe accurately and perfectly knows and understands every single thing about you, including your background and intentions (both good and bad), and still absolutely adores you and is with you at every moment in spite of all He knows…. My goodness, how that sets you free!!! I still don't like that feeling of being misunderstood, but at least I can now walk away smiling to myself and thinking, "It's okay, You know me, Lord!" That makes all the difference in the world and allows you to turn around and reach out to the next person you encounter without the previous experience affecting your self-worth and availability to others. Back when I was a teenager and learning to recognize the Lord's gentle nudging of my spirit, I would drive around and ask Him to show me someone in need. It might be someone with a flat tire or just someone who was alone and needed a kind word, but I always found someone to help. One time it was a mentally handicapped young boy sitting on his porch. It being a more innocent time back then, I stopped my car and went up and sat with him on the porch for a while without fear of being sued. Another time when I was driving through a poor neighborhood, I saw a middle-aged Black woman walking along the road who looked like she was crying. I felt His nudging and drove around the block and came back and pulled alongside her and asked if she was okay. She stopped, looked at me with disdain and said, "I'm all right; are you all right?" and kept walking. I felt so stupid at that moment because she certainly wasn't asking about my well-being; she was asking if I was all right in the head. What can you do except move along feeling like a "perv?"

Things like this still happen to me all the time. I was having breakfast with a very good friend of mine whom I call Beautiful Betty. She really has a beautiful spirit and is always cheerful despite having lost most of her eyesight to macular degeneration. She is almost ninety and never complains or feels sorry for herself, but instead volunteers several days a week at several charitable organizations. We were at a restaurant when I noticed a family nearby who needed more water and was trying unsuccessfully to get the attention of their waiter. We hadn't touched our pitcher so I got up and carried it over, offering to fill their glasses. They stopped talking and looked up at me like I was belching the "Star-Spangled Banner." No thank-yous, not even a polite refusal — just a look of suspicious indifference as they continued their conversation and ignored me as I stood there considering my nonexistent options for dignified withdrawal.

Sometimes I do get tired of reaching out to rude or inconsiderate people, but it has nothing to do with a fear of rejection. It's usually just a sign that I've been running on battery power too long (my own strength) and need to plug directly into my source of Power again (Christ) so I can recharge. This topic points to a clear difference between being a Christian and merely being a "good person." All of us respond with kindness to someone we naturally like and are attracted to, but a true Christian is one who has yielded their life to the point where His Spirit can in-dwell and empower them to love beyond the natural self. I know someone who can do that exceptionally well. They love the unlovable with an authenticity that amazes me, and all without the tendency to tag them as "the least of these." I've actually heard immature Christians do that very thing, even (horrible!) going so far as to say it to that person. To me, that smacks of terrible self-righteousness and false martyrdom, as if they feel the need to advertise just how unlovable a person is and how much effort it requires of them to extend a charitable act. "Why, if Christ hadn't told me I had to do this...."

It is true that some people are hard to love, but it's my hope that others will somehow find a way to love you and me.

Chapter 18

From the Ashes

It's interesting how quickly you settle into whatever conditions you find yourself in. I moved from season to season with relative ease now and adapted to the extreme temperature differences as they came. I had built a lean-to onto my cabin so I could store my firewood out of the weather. The second winter I had run out of firewood too soon and found myself digging in the snow looking for anything to burn. That wouldn't happen again. The next fall, I gathered way more than I could use in one season. I also started using an electric blanket because I often came home too late to start a fire and it was too miserable to do anything but crawl into bed. One frigid night I came home around nine o'clock and the electricity was out. It was below zero inside my cabin; no way was I going to sleep there, so I turned right around and stayed the night with a friend.

Living without water for ten months out of the year certainly had its challenges. I was able to take showers at my sister's home which was only a few miles away, but it wasn't always convenient to go there. Sometimes I would find an empty Y cabin and take my shower there before going up. One September afternoon after the busy summer season had ended,

I was driving toward my cabin and noticed that Timberline Cabin was empty, so I decided to run in and take a quick shower. I went in and took off all my clothes and laid them on the dining table and started the water in the bathroom, when I heard what sounded like a door closing. Oh no, it couldn't be...

I ran to look and through the front window (the curtains were open) I saw a fifteen-passenger van parked beside my truck with loads of people climbing out and onto the front deck. I looked at my clothes — fifteen feet away and right in front of the big window — and had to quickly judge if I could make it or not. What choice did I have? I ran to the table and got my jeans on (no time for underwear!) just as the door opened. I stood there as they pulled up short in surprise and I said, "Hi!" They were actually very friendly and politely asked if I wanted them to come back later. What graciousness! I explained what I was doing there, apologized, and left as quickly as possible. Whew! I always checked with the front desk after that to make sure a cabin was unrented.

The Unveiling

No one at the Y or in Estes even knew that I played guitar. To everyone there, I was "the woodworker." I hadn't picked up my guitar since leaving Waco eight years before and I never talked about it or my musical history. Hearing one song on the radio changed all that. I was listening to a guy from Austin whom I had never heard of and my jaw dropped in disbelief. How was it even possible to play that fast and that cleanly? It was Eric Johnson and the song was "Cliffs of Dover." I immediately bought the cassette and began the monumental task of trying to learn that song. It might be hard to imagine now with variable speed software and looping, but I had to play that cassette to death to even begin to figure out what this maniac was playing! I would start and stop it after two or three seconds and then find it on the fretboard, which was harder and more complicated than just finding the notes like you would on a piano. Any guitarist will understand this challenge because you can usually play the same note and octave in several places, depending on which string you play. For instance, the open note of E (above middle C) can be played in five different positions on a 22-fret guitar. You have to find clues as to the position someone's playing by listening for the highest and lowest note on either side of a scale run. So you might learn the pattern around the fifth fret and then have to totally relearn it in a different position if they unexpectedly play a higher note than you can reach from where you are. All this is infinitely complicated when the player is inhumanly fast like Eric is. It took me a solid month to finally learn "Cliffs," and I had literally worn off the tape's oxide by then. You could barely hear it anymore.

Every year, the Y staff puts on a variety show for the guests and I decided to surprise all my friends by entering. I found out one of the cooks (Craig) played drums and the sound guy (Curtis) played bass so I hooked up with them to premiere this song. The bass player also had a Korg M1 workstation synth and I borrowed it to orchestrate a song of mine that I wrote back when I was fourteen. Digital sequencers were relatively new but I figured it out pretty quickly and created a multitrack background for my finished song, "Snowfall in Vienna." I was able to be exempted from the biweekly rehearsals so no one knew what my act was going to be. Some staff sang, some did comedy, and others acted. My act was a mystery.

I was scheduled to play "Snowfall" near the beginning and then the three of us would play "Cliffs" right after the intermission. I was a little nervous, but not as much as you might expect, especially since it had been nearly a decade since I had played in front of an audience. I looked out during the first acts and I was speechless; it was packed to the gills. Ruesch Auditorium seats over eight hundred people and they were even sitting in the isles! When my turn came, I walked out and was relieved to see that the stage lights only illuminated the first few rows, so it felt like a much smaller audience. One unwelcome surprise came when I realized that the stage crew forgot to bring out my monitor after the last act. This wasn't good at all. I was playing my classical guitar so I sat down and played the intro before starting the keyboard tracks with a footswitch. It was very hard to time my playing with the tracks because I could only hear the echo from the back auditorium wall. Not good at all! I had to play a little softer just to hear my cues. My song was about three minutes long and I was able to get through it without messing up. I ended by myself and the place erupted into applause. Eight hundred people stood on their feet and gave me a standing ovation. I could barely contain the joy I felt after being away from music for so long. I bowed several times, grinning from ear to ear and walked behind the curtain. I was back home.

I was filled with so much adrenaline, I had to walk around and ended up at the top in the back row to watch the following acts and see what the audience perspective was like. Intermission came and we brought out the drums and amps in preparation for opening the second half. I wrote another instrumental, "The Rose of Morning," while I had Curtis' keyboard and opened with that new song when the lights went down. The spotlight was only on me so the audience couldn't see the other two yet. I already had my guitar around my neck so I played the last E chord and sustained it with my foot and launched into the intro to "Cliffs of Dover" on my electric guitar. Craig and Curtis came in right on time and the lights came on full as we played this wonderful, challenging song. During our private rehearsals Craig, the drummer, had struggled with keeping the timing consistent all the way through the song, so I was a little apprehensive about the performance. About halfway through, he started speeding up and I was sweating bullets. This song already pressed me to my absolute limit and here he was speeding up! There was a break for the drums where I played alone and he came back in reasonably close to the original tempo again. We finished with the three of us together and everything pretty much intact. We all received a wonderful response and the stage hands removed our equipment for the next act. We were so excited but also relieved to have it behind us. We could now sit and fully enjoy the rest of the show.

New Identity

The next day was almost surreal as I returned to my normal job making furniture. However, in some ways, my life would never be the same again. All my friends and coworkers now knew me the way everyone back in Texas knew me — as a musician. I was also changed inside as that part of my life which had always been so important to me, came back to the front of my consciousness and reasserted itself as part of my identity. People came up to me every day for the next week, talking about my performance and how shocked they were to find that I played guitar. I had been the cabinet maker for the YMCA for five years now, and nobody had a clue about my musical history until that night.

Once reawakened, there was no going back. I kept playing up in my little cabin and began to entertain thoughts about writing more music and maybe doing a full show. The Y sponsored a summer concert series called Summerfest. Artists had to play for an hour and I was about fifty-seven minutes short. The following year, in 1994, I did something crazy. I booked myself to play at Summerfest. I now had three months to write and record fifty-seven minutes worth of music. I guess I chose this commitment to force myself into getting serious about music again, but I cursed myself almost without end as I headed up to my cabin each day after work so I could try to compose music in preparation for my show. This was especially hard because my close friend, Billy Haney, had been hired to fill Curtis' position as audio visual director. I met him at the airport and got him set up in staff housing, and then had to limit time together to our half-hour lunch each day. This was so hard to do! And then to watch all the new staff come in and not get to participate in any afternoon or evening activities was excruciating. But that's the level of discipline that it took to resurrect my music from its long repose and focus all my energy there again. The day of my show finally dawned and I was excited and nervous because this was all my own original music and I would be the only one on stage this time. If you're a little bit shy like me, it helps to have other distractions for the audience to stare at. All my equipment worked and everything went very well — my first concert featuring my own music was a success. One oddity I noticed was how nerves changed the very character and timbre of my voice. I started morphing into Kermit the Frog during the evening as I spoke between each song. When I relaxed, I began to morph back into my normal voice. We all experience shock the first time we hear our voice on a recording because it sounds so alien. The reason is because your head acts like a resonating cavity and strengthens certain frequencies and harmonics in the lower end, much like bass speakers do when people install them in their car trunk to emphasize the powerful low frequencies found in rap music. We've all heard that thumping bass when stopped at a traffic light, and you can never tell where it's coming from because bass is omnidirectional. But you can usually locate the source after finding the modified racing Honda with smoked glass. So, when you first hear your voice on a recording, it sounds completely tinny because you're hearing it originate outside of your own head cavity. Heady stuff, indeed.

By the time I was ready for my show that summer, two other major events had taken place. My landlord informed me he was getting married and that his new wife would be staying in my cabin(??) so I would have to leave. I didn't ask the obvious burning question, but started looking for a new dwelling. I had been living there for three years now and was ready for a change. Each bill I was able to pay off by staying up there opened up my world of possibilities a little more. I had noticed the cabin across the street often and wondered if it might be available. I found the owners' information and contacted them. Bob and Marcia Taylor said I could rent it for the summer, but nothing beyond that because it wasn't insulated. It was really charming and I looked forward to moving over there when the weather warmed up enough.

New Companion

Felicia and I had kept in touch the whole time and among her many new friends, I kept hearing about one in particular. We had finalized our divorce a couple of years before; oddly enough, I was on my way to a U2 concert in Denver with my friends when I stopped in Boulder so I could sign the papers. Felicia wanted me to meet her good friend, Laura, and thought it would be fun for the three of us to get together for lunch. So we met at a small café in Boulder. I have no idea why I had the impression that she would be blonde and fairly short, but she was just the opposite — tall and brunette. On paper, it sure sounds like it could have been an awkward situation, but it wasn't awkward at all. The conversation flowed easily and there was a lot of laughter. We all felt so good about it that we got together two more times as a threesome and equally enjoyed our time together as her friend and I got to know each other better. We had already heard so much about one other over the last three years that it was like being prequalified for credit. In fact, every time Felicia talked about me to her friend it was in such endearing terms that she wondered why we weren't back together. It may sound strange, but it really makes sense to me. Felicia was on her own journey now, but our friendship and respect for each other were undiminished and so she could speak highly of me, as I did of her. The next time Laura came up to go hiking, she was on her own and called me to see if I would like to go with her. I was excited about it and met her in the parking lot of McDonald's in Estes. Everything still felt very natural and comfortable as we drove into the park for some casual hiking.

The mutual attraction became evident as soon as we were alone but we thought it would be appropriate to ask Felicia how she felt about the idea of us dating. She said she had a feeling all along that we would get on well together and that was her intention in inviting us to meet. So, with a green light in every direction, Laura and I began dating. That same year, my grandmother looked Jesus in the face and became whole after being crippled for ninety-six years on this earth. I want to live a long life and to accomplish as much as possible while I'm here, but there is a part of me that wished I could have been in Heaven already, waiting for Grace to arrive. I wanted to see her jump and shout and take off running as fast as her new immortal body could carry her. For the very first time in her existence, she was free.

Laura, in her incredibly gracious and generous way, used her vacation time to go with Lee Ann, John, and me to bury her next to my mother in the wild mesas around Kenton, Oklahoma. Grace, being ever practical, wanted to be cremated to save us funeral costs, so I used my lathe at work to turn a colorful hardwood urn for her ashes. It was a very sweet time together as we all drove to the small town where my mother grew up. It was great to see our mom's marker again because we hadn't been back since burying her in 1984. Most of my grandmother's friends had already entered eternity so it was a small service, just the way she would have liked it. It's an indescribable feeling, both sad and celebratory, when you say goodbye to those who gave you life and cared for you, and then close that chapter. Peace be unto both of you, until we meet again on a Greater Morning.

Chapter 19

A New Beginning

Love is indeed the strongest force in the universe, but even that has its limits when it's matched up against my living conditions. Laura and I had been dating for six months when we became engaged on Flagstaff Mountain above Boulder, Colorado. She loved to come up and visit me at my cabin, but that's probably only because there was the promise of normalcy awaiting her when she went back to her apartment in Boulder, with heating that you could dial up any old time you wanted, and water that was willing and obedient to your whims and needs. We began to make plans for our wedding and it was pretty obvious that we wouldn't live in my little cabin even if we could, which we couldn't. I was tired of that lifestyle anyway and was ready to move on, so we found a place to rent in Estes Park that was pretty modest compared to other people's homes, but which seemed like a mansion to me after living without heat and running water for four years. It felt like I was coming out of a cocoon, and I was in many ways. I had been critically wounded and retreated into my lair while my Creator restored and rebuilt me once again. I think about the prophet Elijah sitting beside the brook Cherith while ravens brought him meat and drink daily as he regained his strength. I don't know anyone who likes the process of being cared for and fed as you sit on the sideline of life. I welcomed it this time, mostly because it was such a fun challenge and so different from anything I'd ever experienced before while growing up in suburbia. There was one college student who was so enamored with her romanticized image of me as a Mountain Man. I vividly remember her disappointment when I told her I used an electric blanket and not a skin made from a recently killed grizzly.

First Impression Carefully Chosen

On the day I was supposed to meet Laura's parents for the first time, I was refinishing furniture and using a random orbit sander with the hook and loop variety of discs. I was sanding a table leg when the disc flew off the sander and right up into my nose, still happily sanding away. I always wear safety goggles, but that did nothing to protect my schnoz. It's amazing how much skin can come off in a fraction of a second. The angle allowed it to really dig into my nose as it ground its way toward the ceiling. The result was that I had this huge scab covering most of my nose that made me look like Karl Malden. I'm usually very comfortable in my own skin, but not when there's that much of it missing! I just couldn't face making that first impression in this condition. Think about it:

- I'm from Waco (Branch Davidians were fresh on people's minds).
- I'm a musician.
- A *guitarist* at that.
- I'm living in a shack without heat or water.

Be fair! I already had too much against me to arrive with half my nose missing! We rescheduled.

Neither Laura nor I had ever been to Europe before and we started talking about getting married in Switzerland and how much fun that would be. However, when we saw all the restrictions and regulations that would entail, we started thinking about other options. We both liked New England and thought about flying to Boston, but the round-trip airfare alone was $700 each. Then we ran across a newspaper ad in the travel section that offered a package trip to Hawaii. Ten nights total with seven in Oahu and three in Los Angeles, round-trip airfare and accommodations, including tickets to Disneyland. All this cost just around $640 each. We decided that was the place to be, so we loaded up our truck and we moved to Beverly…Hills, that is. Swimming pools, movie stars….

More Than a Feeling

Since both of us had been married before with all the bells and whistles, we felt the freedom to do this on our own without worrying about how far away it was and whether people could make it or not. We bought the packages and started making plans to get married on September 14, 1995. Things started getting interesting when I found out I had suffered a hernia at work. Worker's Compensation would cover it, but I was a little concerned about making the trip and still being able to enjoy myself. The consulting doctor put it like this: "Go ahead and go and enjoy yourself, but just don't parasail or anything like that. If your intestines pop out of the rupture, then you'll have emergency surgery right there." Thank you, and have a great day yourself, Doc.

We got everything packed up for our trip but we were both concerned about my condition, so Laura offered to carry all the heaviest baggage through the airport and in Hawaii when we arrived. I felt bad watching her loaded down like a yak, but I also didn't want to do anything foolish that might jeopardize our honeymoon either. You never think about how far away Hawaii is until you travel there. Five hours from Los Angeles is a big distance! The flight was very smooth and we found our hotel and got settled in. We woke up the next morning and the first thing both of us wanted to do was head to the beach and swim in the ocean. We changed into our swim gear and walked the couple of blocks to the beach. The day was partly cloudy and the ocean felt fairly cool but we had a great time playing around in the water. The first time I dove underwater to examine some of the shells, I came back up and both of my ears were clogged. I couldn't do anything to open them and kept jabbing my finger in my ears trying to bring my hearing back. I couldn't hear squat as we eventually headed back to our hotel to change and then go out sightseeing. We got on a tourist bus and drove all around Honolulu and the surrounding areas, getting off when there was something we wanted to see up close. The problem was, I couldn't hear any of the names the driver was calling out, so I kept standing up, thinking it was time to get off, and Laura would have to pull me down like an over-anxious child.

Up and down, up and down I went like a jack-in-the-box until Laura finally pulled me along by the hand when it really was time to get off. I was starting to feel pretty helpless and humiliated by the end of that day. Then we decided to rent a convertible Mustang and drive up to the North Shore on the other side of the island, where surfing competitions are held each year with some of the biggest waves in the world, sometimes hitting fifty and sixty feet high. My doctor told me not to parasail, but he didn't say anything about jet skis. We each rented a single-seater and took off. It was down-season as far as surfing competitions went but the waves were still pretty big, especially on a jet ski. Our rentals lasted for forty-five minutes and we had a blast flying across the huge designated area. Once I got the feel of mine, I started catching air off the waves. What I didn't realize was that I was unconsciously crouching just above the seat with all the weight on my legs. I only noticed how tired my legs were when our forty-five minutes were up and we turned our machines back in. We climbed back into our car and drove another forty-five minutes to the Polynesian Cultural Center. We found a space in their huge parking lot and I stepped out of the car and immediately fell on my face. Wow, my legs were more tired than I thought! I got up, we started walking toward the entrance, and Bam! Down I went again. This was crazy. I fell several more times before we even got inside, and each time I was finding it harder to get back up. I found that I had to keep my knees locked to stay upright. If they bent even a little bit, I would instantly drop like a sack of potatoes. The worst surprise was yet to come.

Helping Hand

The Polynesian Cultural Center consists of "islands" all separated by arched bridges. Okay, this was bordering on cruel to a man in my condition. There was simply no way to navigate one of these bridges without bending my knees slightly — on both the ascent and descent of the arch. I can't tell you how frustrated it became or how many times I fell, but I finally became so exhausted I couldn't get up again. Humiliation reached a new level when a man in his late seventies had to come over and help Laura get me on my feet again. I'd had occasions before when I swam so much that my leg muscles became truly exhausted and would cramp up constantly; this was something far more extreme. It felt like my thigh muscles had been surgically removed. Laura had to wrap her arm through mine for the rest of our time there to keep me from falling constantly.

I couldn't hear, my herniated intestines were on the verge of breathing the outside air, and now my bride had to lead me around like some organ grinder's monkey. I sure knew how to show a girl a good time!

The rest of our trip was far less traumatic, fortunately. I grew new leg muscles and we made a trip to a local drug store and bought a Waterpik to clean out my ears. This wasn't the souvenir from Hawaii I had envisioned, but it sure was a welcome addition to our possessions at the time, and I still use it occasionally. The important thing was that it worked, and I was able to flush out the seawater-dissolved earwax from both ear canals and hear again! Things were looking up.

Our wedding ceremony took place on Waikiki Beach. We found an ordained priest through a wedding planner that specialized in this kind of wedding and she served as the required witness. The four of us stood barefoot in the sand as we read our vows to each other with the ocean waves providing the music. We enjoyed our wedding day and chose the Chart House for our special dinner that night. It was set up in a beautiful location right on the water and had tropical flowers everywhere. We had reservations and when we came in we must have mentioned that it was our wedding night. The food and atmosphere were delicious and we ate beyond the point of being full; in fact, we were almost miserably full. I had a huge steak and a baked potato with all the trimmings; Laura had shrimp scampi. We both ordered tasty, but filling, strawberry piña coladas, too. We paid our bill and were just getting up to leave when our waiter brought out a towering, complimentary mud pie for our special occasion. We sat back down with a loud thump and thought that we should at least eat a little bit to show our appreciation for their thoughtfulness. We ate every last bite. There's something about dessert that allows you to eat when you couldn't touch another bite of your meal. Neither one of us could believe that we had eaten that whole thing after already being so full; now we truly were in a state as we slowly shuffled back to our hotel several blocks away. Hammer and anvil met in our stomachs and tolled the bell of true misery. We walked past a bar where the band inside was playing Rush and I couldn't even muster enough interest to peek inside. As hard as it was, walking actually helped us as we worked off our enormous meal.

Island Hopping

We decided to fly to the Big Island for a couple of days and take the helicopter tour over Kilauea since it was still gently erupting. For some reason, I was expecting this island to be even more frantically paced and populated than Oahu, but it was refreshingly sparse in population and relaxed in nature. The view over the lava tubes was spectacular, but I was a little thankful when we finally landed. That was my first time in a chopper and the motion is very unpredictable, which unsettled my stomach somewhat. Hawaii is a beautiful island along the coastline but the interior is very dry and desolate, although we stumbled across the occasional oasis as we drove to Hilo. It reminded me of our trip to Mars. Well, it reminded me of the images I'd seen, anyway. It's hard to comprehend the extreme difference in elevation and climate available on the island of Hawaii, but it rises to an elevation of almost 13,800 feet at its highest point, Mauna Kea. It's said to be the tallest mountain on earth if measured from the ocean floor. We didn't make the journey up to see the Mauna Kea observatories on that trip, but I certainly would now. Riding bicycles down from the summit would also be very cool. Oh well, these are excuses to go back again sometime soon.

By the time we flew back to Los Angeles, we had seen so much that neither one of us was interested in going to Disneyland — so we flew back to Colorado early. We came home to five inches of snow on the ground and began a tradition: anytime we went on vacation in September, it was almost guaranteed to snow while we were gone. We had a reception for friends and family within a few days of our return. It's really funny to see pictures of the honeymoon and when we got back because my hair was pretty long at the time and it was curly. Not Brian May-of-Queen curly, but close. I bought my own PA system and enough equipment to start performing live and started booking dates around the Front Range. My rack became so heavy that I needed help loading it in and out of my '87 Toyota 4Runner, which I had recently bought used. I had always loved this particular model and year and now finally I owned one. I had actually saved enough back then to buy one new, but an interesting thing happened — I no longer wanted to part with $15,000 cash. I found it fascinating that I would have been willing to get a loan and spend that much virtual cash, but when it came to handing over the actual, hard-earned "Benjamins," I wouldn't do it. I also had a Honda CRX HF and that was so much fun to drive, but I could barely fit my guitar in there, much less all my other equipment. My three-way JBL speakers, which were three-foot cubes, weighed close to one hundred pounds each — almost as big and heavy as the car itself.

In 1997, I lost one of my close childhood friends and drove that CRX all the way to Waco and then down to Austin and back, and my mileage on that whole trip averaged 66 mpg. I know that sounds hard to believe now, but I kept accurate records and know it to be true. There was a more powerful model called the SI and it "only" got somewhere around 40 mpg, but mine was plenty powerful and I could pass any other car coming up the canyon in third gear. CRX models only weighed around 1,800 pounds, so that was a major reason why they got such good mileage. It was strange switching back and forth between those two vehicles because one felt like a go–cart and the other felt like I was driving a stepladder, such was their difference in height. Paying insurance for both cost too much, so I had to let go of the CRX, which I regret to this day. But the 4Runner was more practical for my needs, so it stayed.

Chapter 20

Home Recording

For the next two years, I continued as the cabinet maker at the YMCA and played shows periodically at night and on the weekends. Recording equipment had come a long way since the days of Studer and MCI 24-track reel-to-reel units, which cost half-a-million dollars. Alesis made a major breakthrough in the early '90s with their eight-track units that recorded onto VHS cassettes. That opened up a lot of opportunities for unsigned musicians to be able to record without spending $100,000 in a major recording studio, but I still didn't like the idea of using tape because of how fragile it was and the maintenance required. Pro Tools had just come out and they allowed you to record onto computer hard disk, but that was brand-new technology and their system cost between $10,000 and $15,000 — way too much for me. By the time 1997 came around, a lot of entrepreneurs had written software that allowed computer recording, and it was improving all the time. I settled on the Akia DR-16 stand-alone unit for about $3,000 and installed a two-gigabyte Seagate hard drive, which cost another $1,200! Now, you can get a four-gigabyte USB drive for a few dollars. Technology always puts the consumer on the losing end because it never stops advancing and making everything you just bought obsolete.

Profound Lesson

I remember a digital synthesizer that was state-of-the-art in the early '80s that sold for close to $40,000. I saw the same unit ten years later in the back room of a music store gathering dust. I couldn't believe I was standing right next to it and asked the salesman if he would mind hooking it up. I had all kinds of mystical, never-heard-before timbres in my head and couldn't wait to fire it up and see what it could do. My disappointment was profound as I heard sounds that were so wimpy now, and not very interesting at any point in time. That experience really taught me a valuable lesson about relative value. I started looking at old cars from the '70s and '80s and imagining the all-consuming lust some people had for those then-exotic machines that were now nothing more than rust buckets with often laughable designs. I, too, often got caught up in the excitement of some new piece of gear that I could feel the almost irresistible pull toward — a pull that would set my mind working on ways to somehow buy it. When I was thirteen, I wanted to own both the AMC Pacer and Gremlin because I thought they both looked so cool. After that experience in the music store, I will never, ever look at anything new the same way again. "Appeal" and "cutting edge" have such a short life cycle, you only have to resist their siren call for a relatively short period of time before the illusion dissipates right before your eyes. That's why television commercials and marketing firms aim directly at your emotions, because there's usually no logical reason to buy the products they sell and they know that. Car commercials are especially vain in this way and they try to make you feel guilty or envious about what your neighbor's driving. They've even started using young children in commercials, who will stop playing ball to stare open-mouthed at some boring new car that you would probably have a hard time finding in a mall parking lot, because it's so unremarkable. That ad is completely laughable, but it almost makes me angry, too, because as ridiculous as it seems, it must be working or they wouldn't spend that much money to produce the commercials. The same principle applies with, "If you call in the next ten minutes...." That one made me laugh at the time, but they're still doing it years later because it obviously works for a certain percentage of the population. Makes you sad if you think about it too much.

My new DR-16 recording deck worked very well, but editing the music on a separate monitor was very cumbersome. It was hard to figure out how to even name the tracks. The Seagate HD was pretty noisy, too, but it was still so exciting to have the freedom and opportunity to record in my own home that I didn't really care about those drawbacks. After working at the Y for the last nine years, I quit so I could pursue music full time. I had custom designed several pieces of furniture and they asked me to come back as a contractor to produce those pieces. So I worked for them a few months a year for six more years. This arrangement was perfect as it gave me most of the year to write and record music.

The Good Life CD

When I had enough songs for an album, I mixed everything down to Laura's Power Mac computer and burned my very first CD in Red Book format. Laura was a graphic artist so she designed and laid out all of the artwork. It's hard to put into words the wonder and pride I felt in producing my own album after dreaming about it for so long. I sent it to the replication house and received the first thousand copies on the very same morning of my show at Summerfest, which was also my CD release party. That was cutting it a little bit too close and I made sure I always had more time for production after that. The response I got was so encouraging, both from the show and from people who bought the CD. I even received phone calls from people around the country telling me how impressed they were and what my music meant to them. Maybe the highest compliment I received was when that girl (Julie G.), who came out and sat beside me on the grass so long ago, listened to it carefully and gave me a song-by-song breakdown and review. She's a talented musician in her own right and also very analytical like I am, so her opinion mattered a lot to me. Her favorite song at the time was "Spire" (and it still is), partly because of the time change that occurs midway in the song.

I began playing up and down the Front Range, even playing at Borders and Barnes & Noble stores as far south as Colorado Springs. The bookstore shows were pretty risky because they didn't pay and you only made as much as you could sell of your merchandise, but I always managed to make at least $100 so they were worth the risk. I didn't do so well at outdoor festivals because my music isn't flashy enough to capture the attention of those walking around, eating cotton candy and looking to buy spice racks. I thought about the singer, Enya, and the horror stories she told about playing in loud environments like bars. And like her, I do best when people are seated and are there to listen; that way I can engage them and draw them in to who I am and the story behind each composition. Another acquisition I quickly discovered I needed was a cart to carry all my equipment on. I played a show at the Fourth Story restaurant located above the old Tattered Cover Book Store complex on Speer Boulevard. This involved parking in an underground garage, traveling all the way through the book store, going up an elevator and then across a walkway to the restaurant. I had to make five trips to get everything in before I could set up and start playing! I ordered a Rock N Roller Multi-Cart as soon as I got back home. That cart really is a lifesaver because it expands and you can get everything in one trip. It's also safer because you don't keep parading all your expensive gear to would-be thieves.

That show was also my first recognition of the challenges you face playing at a restaurant. First of all, most of the diners just want to eat and visit and only hear you as background music. I'm totally fine with that, and in some cases actually prefer it, because you can just relax and play your music. The worst part of it is when you are located at one end of the seating area, because those who are far away complain that they can't hear you, and the ones right next to you complain because it's too loud. Nothing you can do about that unless you have multiple speakers that are summed in mono. No one wants to hear only the Uilleann pipes or acoustic guitar and nothing else — unless you're Irish or a luthier. I often hear CDs and satellite music done that way in local coffee shops or department stores, and am dismayed when I can only hear the Japanese knee trumpet and not the ripping guitar solo on the other side of the store.

Where You Is and Where You Ain't

All gigging musicians on a small scale have stories to tell regarding how people respond to them and their music. Anything from rapturous response to visible indifference can be the result of putting your heart out there in the form of creativity. Some people have hard shells, and others skin of a softer nature, but everyone has to learn to deal with being accepted and rejected simultaneously. Some composers write with the sole objective of scoring hits and making a lot of money while others create purely from the heart and imagination — and often suffer the consequences of their daring. A small percentage are able to do exactly what they want and somehow find a worldwide audience to support them in their career. I think of Peter Gabriel and Kate Bush as being some of those exceptions. Peter already had an established fan base from his days with Genesis and he carried enough momentum from that period to transition into his solo projects without too much loss — then built an even larger audience from there. Kate may be one of the rarest examples in that she was discovered by a family friend — who just happened to be David Gilmour, the guitarist from Pink Floyd — and then protected and nurtured by her record company until she was old enough and mature enough to not be harmed by the experience. Can you imagine that happening today? Childhood prodigies are now captured and drained of their money-making essence like a dairy cow on an industrialized farm.

Entertainment and success are virtual targets in constant motion. You need to have the constitution and drive of a Mongol conqueror to have any hope of surviving (much less achieving a high level of success) in this industry, while still keeping your relationships and integrity intact. It's the same with acting: only the stout of heart need apply here. It takes all-out commitment and sacrifice to reach the top, and I don't think I ever had that killer drive. The rest of my life, including relationships and other interests, were too important to leave behind in a pure pursuit of success. You also have to be a shameless self-promoter to be able to get your name out there and be recognized out of an increasingly growing crowd of people who are trying to do the same thing, and I stink at that. Don't get me wrong, I have an ego too, and face the same challenges at whipping and taming that misplaced ferocious lion as everyone else does who is in the public eye. The key is to be honest and accurate in your assessment of who you really are and what you want to do. If you're footloose and fancy free and willing to do anything to "make it", then buy a van and good luck to you! If you're anywhere short of that intensity, then discern what will make you happy and be satisfied and content with that. I can't stress how important it is to have your own definition of "success." If you are motivated by the definitions of others, then you face a long, frustrating, and never-ending journey through this life. What's actually worthy of your time and attention in this life is another topic entirely.

As a follower of Christ, what I do in private is just as important as what I do in public. Even more so in light of what Jesus said about receiving the praise and attention of others for good works, as opposed to showing kindness in small ways that go unnoticed by everyone except God. This view changes your whole perspective about what's important in this life, and hopefully sets you free to spend your time on the things that are of value in Heaven, and not on temporary indulgences and possessions that you will lose when you die.

Grounded

So where was my relationship to Christ and church at this point in my life? I still believed and was walking within sight of Him, but without the comforting and life-giving intimacy that should be our daily experience. I had no desire to be involved in church at all, or to surround myself with other believers. I didn't avoid them, but I certainly didn't seek them out. I knew some wonderful Christians, too, but my heart and mind were currently filled with the experiences of those whom I felt were way too narrow-minded and "churchy." There's a whole world out there full of beauty and interest that have legitimate value, and church to me at that time felt like shutting all that out and living in a closet. Secular music was far more interesting and creative than anything I heard in Christian music, where they often just copied whatever was currently popular and then produced their version of it. That disgusted me, and still does if I'm completely honest. It should be the other way around. The children of the Creator should be the ones leading the way — not just in music, but in every area of life. To look at the incredible diversity in the ocean alone, and then compare that to what was being produced in His name, filled me with incredulous shame. Please understand that I'm not belittling Christendom and all who dwell there, I'm just trying to reveal where my heart and rebellion was at the time. I wanted to be out there writing and performing in any venue that would have me, and in my own subtle way, share and express my core belief that we are made in His image and have a purpose here and a hope of Life beyond this one.

One of the reasons I love C. S. Lewis so much and respect him as an author and as a man, is because he was so damned honest. (Hey, if you're going to have a potty mouth, take it outside!) In his autobiography, he shared his belief that God walked right alongside him during his rebellion and atheism (although his friend, J. R. R. Tolkien, accused him of simultaneously being angry at God for not existing). Lewis believed God was teaching him how to worship (even false idols) for the day He would call him back to Himself. If that's true, which I believe it is, how unspeakably gracious He is to use elements of our rebellion against Himelf, for our good and for His greater purpose later on. Leslie Phillips, in her song "Your Kindness," sang, "It's your kindness that leads us to repentance, oh Lord. Knowing that you love us, no matter what we do, makes us want to love you, too." That's brilliantly said and so true in my own life and experience. When I sense Him raising his hand and I find myself cringing and expecting the blow to be delivered, I discover it was only to caress me instead. He certainly disciplines us, too, but it's still out of His love. To ask Him to leave us alone is to ask for the very worst fate that we could ever imagine.

Even as I was running up and down the Front Range performing and selling CDs, two other roads were quickly converging on me.

Chapter 21

God Loves the Impossible

Since buying my land in 1990, there were a couple of times that I came close to selling my two acres, but fortunately I was smart enough to hold on even when I despaired of ever building anything on it. It's humbling to look back and see how things lined up without my being aware of it. My purpose in moving to Maine was to learn how to design and build my home and it ended up being a disappointment in that regard, but that wasn't the end of the story. My job as cabinet maker, and those I was privileged to work with during my nine years at the YMCA, taught me far more than I could have learned in school. After a year of doing music, Laura and I both felt like it was time to investigate the possibility of building our home. I now owned the land free and clear and we began sketching rough floor plans. Laura, with all her computer skills, preferred pencil and paper, and I used a cheap CAD (computer-aided design) program to lay out my ideas on her Power Mac. We went through a lot of incarnations, ranging from living quarters over a garage, to much more extravagant designs. We wanted to keep it relatively simple, but the twenty percent grade of our property dictated a few parameters and characteristics of what we would need to design and build.

Intangibility

I had made sure that the property I bought faced south because I wanted solar exposure to be part of the overall heating plan. We also have a stream that bisects the property and the north facing section on the other side is too steep to build on easily, so that eliminated a pretty good percentage of the two acres right from the start, along with the fact that our road frontage is pretty minimal, which dictated where the driveway would have to be. Mountain properties also have a much more generous setback requirement than suburban and newer developments have. As Laura and I measured out potential footprint areas, it became clear that there were only a couple of possibilities. With everything we learned, and seeing how quickly our plans were taking shape, we made the commitment and found a place to rent about a mile away from the property. I did a lot of research, found a much better CAD program, and decided I could make the blueprints myself. After a lot of variations and adjustments, we found the right combination of form and function, priority and compromise, and I started the arduous but very fulfilling challenge of laying out all the walls in the detailed drawings that our building code required. As I write this, I'm almost overwhelmed by all that we did and accomplished just to get the process started. I first had to apply for and submit a Site Plan Review, which had nothing to do with the blueprints and house design. This was simply the layout of the property and where specific things were located along with our proposed building site. I was able to do my own percolation test to determine the soil content and drainage rate for our septic system and leach field. We didn't have to do a soil analysis test, but our neighbors who started their site plan process just a month later, did have to. They were not allowed to do their own percolation test, either. Boulder County is notorious for making life difficult for builders. They don't want to see a blade of grass displaced if it isn't absolutely necessary. This poor couple across the street had to spend tens of thousands of dollars before a shovel ever hit the dirt. Part of this was their own fault because they submitted plans for a 14,000-foot home, which broke the plane of the sky, meaning their home would rise above the surrounding ridgeline behind them. That really complicates matters and they had to hire a surveyor to come out and shoot perspective from each of the neighbors who would see their home. Our hearts went out to them.

Only those who have designed and built their own home can understand how overwhelming all the details and preparations are. I knew enough to at least get myself into trouble and now had the confidence to feel sure I could learn whatever I needed to meet any challenge that I encountered. The site plan process took far longer than we anticipated, which made it look like we would have to start building in late fall. Meanwhile, I was able to finish all the blueprint page requirements and submit the e-files to a local engineering firm to have them printed. There were only a few details that required an engineer's stamp, so the inspection process actually went quite well, considering that this was our first time to do any of this stuff. There were a few compromises that we had to concede, like moving the building spot closer to the road by thirty feet. They were convinced that it would be more level up there. As it turned out, it was within an inch of our original location. That change was actually for the better because our driveway would be shorter with less snow to blow clear during the winter. I also had to rotate the house seventeen degrees from due south because of height restrictions. That lowered the solar gain slightly, but it was worth it because they would have required us to hire a surveyor otherwise, to make sure our house was under thirty-five feet from the existing grade. I installed the meter and electrical box on the pole at the top of where our driveway would be and Mike Mangelsen, the Utility Director for Estes Park Light and Power, came out to inspect it. He added an extension for the overhead mast where the wires came across the street, but otherwise approved everything I had done.

Breaking Ground

Our site plan was approved and A-1 Excavating brought their equipment in to start building our driveway. After eight years of sitting alone on my property and dreaming about where my house would sit and what the views would look like from the living room, the sight of that equipment starting to move rock and dirt was overwhelming. It was really beginning to happen! It was both extremely exciting and extremely intimidating because we had secured a construction loan from a local bank in Estes and had to immediately withdraw $40,000 to cover those initial costs. It's one thing to work on your own private project, but when you start involving others and incurring expenses on that scale, it transfers the weight of responsibility right onto your shoulders. At a certain point, I would have to take over and I had better be prepared and know what I was doing, step-by-step. We would have an unfinished walk-out basement, but I wanted all the plumbing to already be in place when we decided to finish it. So I read up on what I would need to know about code and bought all the necessary pipe and connections that would be buried under the basement slab and began laying it all out in our rental's front yard to make sure I had everything correct for the necessary drainage grade and pitch. I also had to prepare a smaller assembly to place under the garage slab to help drain the water from snow melt when we pulled our vehicles in.

All the crews were fantastic to work with, and many of the workers were already friends of mine, so it was even more fun to see them participating in what had once seemed like an unattainable dream. These being the Rocky Mountains, you don't just bring in an excavator and dig up dirt. This was fractured granite, so they had to drill lots of deep holes to place dynamite in and break everything up before it could be removed. Chris Eshelman and Tim Johnson were friends of mine who did this. It was such hard work but both men had the physique and endurance to accomplish it. Unfortunately, I was gone on the day they blasted so I didn't get to see all the fireworks. Pretty soon they had everything cleared and prepared for the foundation to be formed and poured. The excellent men of Mountain Concrete came in to do this and I was so impressed with their ability to calculate and measure the footprint to within one-quarter of an inch diagonally. The footprint was 66' x 24', and it was even more impressive considering the twenty percent grade they had to take into account for their calculations in placing the wall forms. Watching the pumper truck come in and pour the concrete walls was amazing! I couldn't imagine the horsepower it took to lift and push that much weight up, over, and into the forms. Once the concrete had cured enough, they came and took the forms down and then prepared to pour the slabs.

I stepped in at this point and dug up the channels so I could place the plumbing assemblies in the ground. It took a while to get the grade correct, but once it was done and inspected, they could get ready to pour. Building in the mountains can be very difficult because of the unpredictable weather and temperature changes. Everything was ready to pour the slabs now, but the meteorologists were calling for a major drop in temperature as an arctic front came through. "Major drop" meant a fifty-degree difference and it was forecast to be negative-sixteen degrees that evening. We all talked about it and decided to go forward on this December day and hope for the best. These guys really know what they're doing so I trusted their judgment and experience at these elevations (8,500 feet). Once again, my respect soared as I watched them pour, shovel, level, and finish our two slabs. You could really feel the temperature rapidly dropping and they covered the finished slabs with insulated tarps to hold in the heat produced during the curing process. Cinder blocks were added to help hold them in place.

Night Shifts

We can get very fierce winds during the wintertime but it's usually calm when it snows or during very cold weather. Not this time. By that evening, it was gusting up to fifty miles per hour and we stood by and watched as the tarps opened up to reveal the vulnerable concrete beneath. At negative-sixteen degrees, it would quickly freeze and turn into a huge crumbly mess if we couldn't keep it covered. So Laura and I ran around that night pulling the tarps back in place and adding large rocks and anything else we could find to help weigh them down. When it's windy here, it's almost always violent and swirls in different directions as it tries to navigate all the mountain ridges surrounding us. It was very frustrating and stressful as we tried everything possible to protect the concrete from freezing only to see it all open up again, sending the rocks and cinder blocks sliding across the surface like a friendly game of curling. This was not friendly at all and we were acutely worried for several days, fully expecting to see the first signs of the inevitable damage. None occurred at all. And even though we were still concerned over the next few weeks, we finally began to relax and give thanks to God for protecting it.

The wind and the snow both became our bitter enemies as I began to place the first pressure-treated lengths of sill plate on top of the poured walls. Laura was working full time so I was usually alone as I began framing. Even building the first wall across the southern part of the basement was made hard by the constant gusty wind. I couldn't even stand on a ladder and extend my tape measure down to the ground without it being bent and ripped from its tenuous hold. I had all the sill plates in place and the basement wall finished when Laura came over after work. As frustrating as it was, it still felt so good to actually be doing the work and building my dream fifteen years after first conceiving of it. Even though I was fully immersed in framing and reaching a new high in my confidence level, I also found a part of myself standing back and observing this miracle as if from a distance. How did I get here from that troubled, hopeless young teenager? I remembered sitting in my room at age eleven and running my fingers across a contoured plastic map of Colorado and wishing with all my heart that I could one day live there in those breathtaking mountains. It felt no different than wishing I could jump off my front porch and land on the moon; it felt that far away and just as unrealistic. What had God done in my heart and life that actually allowed this to be happening for real?

All those cold, lonely nights in my little cabin above the Y began to make sense and feel worth it. All the sacrifices began to form in my mind as an achievement and the necessary steps that helped lead me to the realization of this goal. I never really thought of myself as being goal-minded while I was growing up, but I started to believe that I could do anything I set my mind to, insofar as it depended on me. This felt revolutionary and it empowered my soul to imagine beyond what I thought I was even capable of. How on earth did I get here? The pleasure of feeling and hearing a nail sink into wood took on a whole new intensity as stud after stud went into place and formed the walls that would one day surround and protect us from these same elements I was joyously suffering in now. Here I am, writing this book fifteen years later as my Jotul Oslo wood stove gently warms me with the firewood I felled and gathered with my twenty-four-year-old Stihl chainsaw. Heavenly Father, You are amazing.

Chapter 22

Building the Dream

The interior walls of the basement had been a challenge even though I was somewhat protected from the worst of the wind. I couldn't imagine what was waiting for me when I came out of hiding. Providence was with me at strategic points and I was able to place all the TJI floor joists in relative calm. This was really starting to look like something now as I began placing the three-quarter-inch subfloor. People often have celebrations of some kind when their first floor is done but before any other walls are up, and I was greatly anticipating that moment when we could walk around on our flat, spacious platform and see the view of Meadow Mountain from our future living room.

There was no wind, but it was late afternoon when I was trying to decide whether or not to cut the banding around a bunk of structural waferboard. I figured I would have time to at least lay a few sheets down before calling it a day, so I decided to open it. The next morning I was driving to the property when I saw something peculiar; all the trees had some kind of trash stuck in them. There's a small rise on the road that leads to our property and I kept seeing more of this stuff as I crowned the top of the rise and more of the scene came into view. As I drove closer, the "trash" resolved itself into much larger chunks and a suspicion began growing in my mind. At the top of our driveway, I realized what I had been seeing wasn't trash at all, but huge sections of the three-quarter-inch waferboard. The wind had come up in the night and peeled off sheet after sheet from the bunk like cards from a deck and threw them twenty feet in the air and into the trees, shattering most of the 4' x 8' sheets into many pieces. I couldn't believe my eyes: this was structurally engineered subflooring that could support any live load you would find in a residential setting, including a grand piano! This gives you some idea of the ferocity of the wind we have up here. I parked and began to scout the area, finding half and full sheets scattered everywhere over our two acres, even all the way down into the stream. The rest of the morning was spent retrieving all that I could from the trees and the stream and trimming them to salvage as much as possible.

By the end I was able to make use of at least eighty percent of what had been damaged, so I was very thankful for that, but I certainly learned my lesson. It didn't matter if it was calm, I would assume hurricane force winds would come from then on and tie everything down securely before leaving the site. When I opened other bunks of material, I would drive three-inch screws into each corner before leaving, and the additional weight of having four sheets together prevented the wind from having its way anymore. We didn't have a large block party or anything too grandiose, but Laura and I did enjoy a couple of cold Dr Peppers and some snacks when we finished that first level on a fairly warm and sunny day.

Virtual Walls

Now it was time to start framing the gable ends and side walls that would support the second level. Most framers use chalk to lay out and measure the stud length for gable walls, but since I was using a very accurate software program, I figured I could just do it on the computer and then print it out. It worked perfectly and I could virtually build each gable end and see the length of each stud to an accuracy of one-sixteenth of an inch or even finer if I needed it. I had designed a 12/12 pitch for our roof (twelve-inch rise for a twelve-inch run) and so I could confidently cut each stud at forty-five degrees, knowing that everything would fit together perfectly when assembled. But first, I framed the long side walls and then called friends over to help raise them. Once all those walls were in place and secured with bracing, I framed the largest west gable wall, which was twenty-one feet high. Engineers calculated the wind load and determined that two full-length microlams (laminated beams) would be required, so I had to frame it all as one piece with openings and headers in place. I also sheathed it on the outside while it was flat on the floor. The result was very large indeed.

I had toenailed the bottom plate so it would act as a hinge when we raised it. Remember the story about finding myself on that one-hundred-foot cliff and fearing for my life? The exact same thing happened again. My father-in-law, Gary Martin, who was a superintendent for one of the largest building contractors in the country, had been coming up from Boulder to help since he was now retired. Gary and Dan D'Amico, a friend and neighboring artist who paints for a living, happened to be there on the same day. Three grown men standing around a construction site can lead to dangerous scenarios. Why? Because all men like to test their strength, and the three of us stood there looking at that wall just a little too long. We started innocently enough by just wondering how heavy that beast was. "Well, let's lift it a little bit and see." So we positioned ourselves evenly and raised it to waist height. Hmm, it's not that bad, we all said, and without verbally making a decision started lifting it higher. We raised it over our heads and still felt okay, so we started walking under it, and that's when we began to tire. Remember, the side walls were already in place and they now created even more drag as we pushed the gable wall past them. We were also losing leverage as we moved closer to the fulcrum, and began carrying more and more of the total weight. In the beginning, we were only lifting half the weight, but that changes as you walk farther under it.

Attack of the Killer Wall

By the time we had it at about a 45-degree angle, we realized that we were all pretty exhausted and couldn't lift it any higher. In the same way that I realized my foolishness on that cliff, we realized our mistake in trying to fully raise it; we now also had nothing with which to support the wall. We started trying to walk backward and slowly lower it, but that only increased the weight because the momentum and pull from gravity made it heavier and harder to control, plus we were already exhausted. We were stuck, and every minute we stood there drained us further. At one point our exhaustion became too great and we had to quickly turn around and support the wall with our backs and place our arms on our knees to form a small triangle. I started thinking about the 5.5″

x 14.5″ space between each stud and wondered if I could fall into that small area when the wall came crashing down. Unfortunately, even if I was lucky enough to have the studs land on either side of my shoulders, I was definitely more than 5.5 inches in thickness and I would still be crushed because I had also glued the sheathing as well as nailed it in place. I felt like I was looking at death once again, and this time, I would be taking my father-in-law and neighbor with me.

There just "happened" to be a carpet installer next door and his son just "happened" to be outside playing and close enough to hear our voices and know that something was wrong. He came over and we started asking for help. He quickly located a 2″ x 6″ and propped it under one of the wall cavities beneath a window header. We tested it hesitantly and it seemed to hold, so we collapsed onto the deck and began crawling out from under it in case the brace gave way. We were literally seconds away from letting the wall collapse and probably kill us when that young man in his early teens saved our lives with his quick thinking. My father-in-law crawled to his car and went home early. My neighbor had to go to physical therapy a couple times over the next week, and I spent a couple hours at home recuperating before I went back and added more bracing. That was a close call, and a dangerous situation we walked right into without recognizing the potential for it, and preparing ahead of time as we should have. We later calculated the weight of that wall to be around 1,800 pounds.

The west gable wall sat there at a 45-degree angle for a couple of days until I could buy a reel of steel cable that we could fasten around a large tree in the distance. I had a come-along that we wrapped through the window openings and then attached to the cable, and we began slowly cranking the wall up. Every few feet, we would have to stop and reposition the bracing so we could feed out the short length of come-along cable and then crank it up a few more feet. We had to repeat this cycle several times before it was finally in place. My father-in-law was feeling better by then and he came back up and brought his son, Mark. Laura was also there and together we secured "The Monster" with nails and permanent bracing. Then we called it an early day and went to a restaurant to celebrate our victory.

Chains Equal Peace of Mind

Having seen what the wind could do, traditional bracing wasn't enough in my mind, so I attached half-inch eyebolts at various places along each wall and deck and chained everything in place. As our home rose higher and higher above the ground, so did the exposure and risk from the wind. I don't know how many times I came out in the middle of the night to make sure the walls were still standing over the next few months, but it was a lot. If I heard the wind come up during the night, I couldn't get back to sleep without knowing everything was okay. There were a couple of times that this saved us from losing a wall because the wind had sheared the nails attaching the braces and I was able to reattach them. After building all the interior walls on the first floor, I installed the second floor joists and laid the subfloor for our master bedroom and bath. Building and raising the other two gable ends was a piece of cake compared to raising the west gable wall that nearly took us out. We didn't have knee walls so those gables merely consisted of isosceles triangles that were twelve feet high. My friend, Ole Sykes, came over and we raised and secured them both on one windless afternoon.

Now that everything was in place and braced with both wood and chains, it became a major hassle to clear around them when we got snow. And snow it did! We normally average around 144 inches each year, but that particular winter, it snowed 121 inches in just two months! It seems like we spent half the morning each day just trying to clear the overnight snow. Laura would shovel the driveway so we could receive the next lumber delivery, and I spent my time clearing the floors so I could work.

My design called for a T-shaped ridgeline so that was the next step. Mike's Welding made me a custom hanger that would receive the fifty-five foot ridge beam from the west wall as well as the two valley beams. After placing the shorter ridge of the "T," I had to quickly install the rafters on the east side to keep the beam up there. We couldn't use pre-made scissor trusses because we would have lost too much headroom on the second floor, and adding knee walls to increase our headroom would have caused us to exceed our total height restriction on the outside. So the only solution was to hand-build the roof using 2″ x 12″ lumber. This caused the roof construction to take much longer than if we could have just hired a crane and installed trusses. After the eastern rafters were in place, I attached the custom bracket and prepared three kick jacks as we waited for another calm day.

One Day – One Beam

When that day dawned, Laura and I maneuvered the four-hundred-pound, fifty-five-foot ridge beam onto the second floor. It was 3½″ wide by 16″ deep and very hard to lift and thread through the eastern rafters. Once the ridge beam was on the second level, we pushed half of it out over the living room and onto two of the kick jacks. Then began the very slow process of lifting that beam twenty-two feet into the air so that it could sit on top of the west gable. I would have to kick it up a few feet on one end, climb down and go to the other kick jack, and raise it a few feet to keep it level, then repeat the process over and over. When we had it high enough to sit on top of the gable, we had to use my come-along to pull the beam horizontally into the hanger pocket. The whole process took six hours just for that one beam — and I had to move really fast now. If the wind came up, fifty-five feet of unsupported beam would begin to flex back and forth until we lost it. The day before, I had already prepared several rafters to immediately install as soon as the beam was in place. I put in two rafters midway and then began to breathe a sigh of relief as I installed the rest of the rafters.

Putting in the valley beams was another matter entirely. They were about the same dimension as the long ridge beam, but I had to gang two of them together — side-by-side — and then fasten them with glue and a specific pattern of nails because of the additional dead load they would carry from each valley rafter. This made the valley beams extremely heavy and difficult to manage when I raised one end to sit in the hanger pocket, inclining them more than thirty degrees. I had to pick one end up and climb twelve feet up the ladder to reach the hanger while holding it against my side. The higher I climbed, the steeper the angle became and the more the beam tried to slide off the edge of the roof. Laura would sit on the edge with her feet placed against a temporary brace to help hold it while I lifted and placed it, securing it with a few nails from my nail gun. This was probably the most vulnerable and dangerous time for Laura. She had very specific directions to just let go and roll away if I yelled. I didn't want her to get crushed or be pulled over the edge with it if something went wrong. I miscalculated the first bird-mouth cut and we had to bring it back down so I could correct it. After that, everything went smoothly and we were able to get them in place and secured.

Once all the valley rafters were in place, I began sheathing the entire roof, starting with the edges so each sheet above could have something to rest on. The building code required a one-sixteenth-inch space between each sheet so they could have room to expand on the hottest days. I placed temporary nails at each end to provide that gap and then glued down each sheet with liquid nails in addition to using ring-shanked fasteners. I knew what the winds were like up here and I wasn't planning on losing anything! The problem with leaving a small gap between each sheet was that rain and snow melt could drip right into the living space all around the house. I don't think other builders left that much of a gap and I don't think I would either if I ever built another one. Because of that, it took us a long time to get it dried in and many of the edges on the subfloors had to be sanded flat because they started to lift due to the continued exposure to moisture. Note to self: pay more and use CDX plywood next time…

I tell you, walking around in our master bedroom when it finally became three-dimensional (with all the rafters in place) was one of the highlights of my whole experience in building our home. It was absolutely thrilling. We were never completely satisfied with our master bathroom layout because of the limited headroom from the rafters. One day as we were walking around in that space, Laura came up with an excellent improvement and I went ahead and changed the interior wall placement according to her spontaneous design. It didn't involve any load-bearing walls, so I didn't think Boulder County building inspectors would have a problem with the bathroom being different from our blueprints — at least I hoped they wouldn't! I also added several skylights on our loft and master bedroom that weren't part of the blueprints. They came out, looked everything over, and passed it without saying a word about the changes. Whew!

Chapter 23

Where Clouds Are Born

Building your own home is an incredible privilege, but it is also incredibly stressful. Owner-builders are considered very high risk because of the high rate of defaults; they either run out of money or get frustrated and lose interest. This was my dream and I was putting everything I had into it, and so was Laura. She would come out after work each day and help in any way she could, and we both worked on weekends. The bank that held our construction loan was monitoring our every move and the vice president would often come out to check our progress — and to offer "motivational" speeches. This became pretty irritating after a while because we were already starting to work seven days a week on our own initiative, and would continue that pace for the last seven months. He really couldn't say anything to pressure us more than we were already pressuring ourselves. When we started asking him if he had brought his hammer, he would snicker and then be on his way. He was actually a pretty nice guy, but he couldn't let go of that inner need to try and push us, which was totally unnecessary. Expenses add up quickly when you're building a house and our construction loan interest was at ten percent. That in itself would have pushed us along because we wanted to finish as quickly as possible and then get a more reasonable rate through a first mortgage.

Because the grade of our property was so steep, the south-facing roof required me to carry the 4' x 8' sheets of OSB (Oriented Strand Board) up through the rafters. Trying to balance a full sheet on your back with one hand while climbing twenty-one feet in the air isn't easy. I dropped more than a few, especially as I grew tired over the course of the day. A really interesting event happened when it finally came time to place the last piece. Since I could no longer go out through the rafters, I had to lean the ladder up against one of the gables and carry the last piece along the ridge line, straddling the roof like a really big horse. It was a very slow process, but with no wind, it was manageable. My father-in-law had threatened violence against me if I didn't set up a one-quarter-inch safety line earlier in the process of building. Since it was already installed, I put on my harness to carry up that last piece, which was about four feet square. I finally reached the area and was about to place it when a big gust of wind came out of nowhere and blew me off the peak. It happened so quickly, I didn't even have time to let go of the plywood, and it acted like a parachute, carrying me off of my wooden horse and down the roof toward a twenty-foot drop. For some reason, I had also worn my hard-shell knee pads and I was so thankful I did! There was a lower gable just above the edge and I hit the peak hard with my knees before the safety line caught and flipped me around violently. I'm sure I would have fractured my kneecaps without those pads.

Widow Maker

Laura's father, Gary, also came out as often as he could to help and was invaluable. After I had all the walls up, he made arrangements for us to borrow enough scaffolding to create two 3-story towers. Then I bridged them with what he called the "widow maker" — a wooden I-beam I made from two 24-foot TJIs. We had originally planned to finish the outside with manufactured river rock — the same kind that I would use to build a 21-foot wall behind our wood stove. Fortunately, the company had become extremely popular and couldn't keep up with demand, so we had to go with an alternative. I say fortunately because it would have been an extended nightmare if the rock had been available. First of all, I had never done much masonry work and it would have taken me a long time with the amount of square footage we had to cover. The other problem was our altitude and weather, which would have required us to cover all the walls with plastic sheets to protect them from moisture, and then, in addition, place heaters underneath to prevent the mortar from freezing. Trying to do that with seventy-mile-an-hour winds is almost impossible — and dangerous as well. I found a company called James Hardie who made patterned cement board in 4′ x 10′ sheets and we decided to go with that. Gary would often call me first thing in the morning to ask what the weather was doing and if he should come up. I would be yelling into the phone, "No! It's a bloody hurricane up here!" He would say that was ridiculous because it was calm down there in Boulder. An hour later he would show up and then ask why I hadn't told him it was so bad. Most of the time he would have to turn around and head right back down. That's the problem with mountain weather; a snow squall might come in with high winds and create whiteout conditions, and then clear up two hours later. You just never knew, and there were many times when I would pack up my equipment, thinking it was over for the day, only to see blue appear a short time later and have to go back out. Good thing we only lived a mile away.

Laura used her vacation time to help me wrap our home in Tyvek and and then install the cement panels. They were only five-sixteenths of an inch thick but they were extremely heavy and very hard to machine. I had to buy special diamond-coated circular saw and jigsaw blades to cut them. With the exception of one panel that broke in half as we lifted it into place over a large window opening, everything else went up without mishap over the next two weeks. After trimming out the exterior, I could now begin working on the inside. I had built our hearth and was now laying rock on the big wall behind it. The frost line is very deep at this altitude and so they had to place our water pipe seven feet deep. This required a lot of blasting and I wasn't very happy with the timing. Every time a charge went off, the deep rumble shook the house and I looked at my freshly laid rock just waiting for half of it to fall. Fortunately, I never lost a piece but my blood pressure must've been high for a few days. I also discovered something else about myself that I wasn't happy with at all. I thought I had already dealt with anger and cursing when I was fifteen, when the Lord rebuilt me from the inside out. Now I learned the ugly truth: those kinds of things are never truly dead, but only dormant in submission to your will. And your will is only strong when empowered by a force outside of yourself. Remember, I had walked away from Christian fellowship nine years before, and though I still believed, the protection that comes with a close and personal walk with Christ and other believers was gone. Nature hates a vacuum, and in the absence of something better, those uglier sides of human nature crept back in, at least in the case of anger and cursing. I never got mad at any person but I soon developed an unquenchable inferno toward inanimate objects. Once you let the beast out of the cage, it wants to run, and run it did! I'm sure a major part of it was the pressure and responsibility I felt from building this house, and the weather certainly didn't contribute to putting a smile on my face. Most of these outbursts came when I was alone, but there were occasions when Laura had to endure it. As always, she was gentle and comforting, but also concerned for my safety as I stomped a careless path in my unrighteous indignation. I was often dancing on the ragged edge of disaster already, as all those who work construction are, and it wouldn't take much in the way of decreased coordination to push me over the edge, literally. Toward the end, I had a pretty light trigger and a casual scratch on the surface could release the molten magma waiting just underneath.

Angry Bird

One day when I was alone, the demonic air hose that fed my nail gun became entangled on the main floor out of pure spite and active malice. Oh yeah?? I'll show you who's boss! I yanked that hose with superhuman strength and out of the cave it came like a roaring tiger, hitting me just above my left eye, which was unprotected at the moment. The heavy brass coupler smashed into my temple from twenty feet away and dropped me to my knees in pain. My anger quickly drained away as I realized how close I had come to putting my own eye out. This was another painful lesson, but one that carried potentially serious consequences if I didn't master it quickly. I really was surprised and ashamed to see how far down I had slipped over the years. I also realized that nothing is truly static in the universe. Everything is always in motion and we as human beings are always either moving toward God or away from Him. There's no such thing as a neutral position, as much as we would like to think otherwise. Every choice and action we take is either healthy or unhealthy for us, and affects others either positively or negatively. Accountability isn't something any of us accepts easily and is one of the major stumbling blocks we have to get over in coming to believe and trust in God. That and pride.

I say the weather didn't put a smile on my face, but that isn't entirely true. I can recall countless times when I would have liked nothing better than to just sit down and watch how clouds literally came into being right before my eyes. We can see the Continental Divide close up and the vapor in the air would compress against the mountains and condense into visible mashed potatoes. I wanted to pour gravy over them and chow down — at least visually. I had never lived anywhere like this before, where the weather and cloud formations were so dynamic. They were fascinating and I longed to have the freedom to watch this amazing show. Equally impressive were the massive lightning storms that formed in the northeast toward Fort Collins. Sometimes we could hear them and sometimes they were silent. Both phenomena were totally hypnotic, especially when the discharges were intense, happening every second and illuminating the interior of the anvil clouds towering overhead. I have always been a weather buff and amateur meteorologist, and this was a dream location to observe from. It often hails where we live, but it is of a softer kind — kinder and gentler than what it will mature into in a matter of a few miles east of here. As far as I know, there has never been a funnel sighting in Allenspark, even though the experts say it's possible in theory. Our location reminds me of an early scene in *Raiders of the Lost Ark*, where Indiana Jones accidentally triggers that giant round stone and is chased to the front of the cave, jumping out and narrowly escaping. I always thought that if he had just taken a few steps forward — toward the stone, it would have passed right over his head and he would have been safe. We are in that safe place where the developing storm passes overhead and gains the power and destructive strength that will lash the countryside from Lyons on eastward. I have a live-radar app that shows a storm's progress in real time and how a system moves from orange to red to purple, sometimes even becoming a supercell out on the plains that will spawn tornadoes.

I wanted to sit and observe, but I couldn't yet. I still had to finish my dream and then go around and apologize to our new neighbors for the mysterious voice that thundered out curses over the beautiful hills. Of course, they were all very gracious and most said they didn't even hear anything out of the ordinary. A man living in the mountains can take that two ways. I found and ordered thirteen 55-gallon black plastic drums from a Y2K website. They must have thought I was either expecting the end of the world or filling them with my homemade moonshine. They were actually for the much more benign purpose of being filled with water to store heat from our southern exposure. I placed them down in the walk-out basement where they would collect BTUs from the sun and then release them back into our basement at night. The heat would naturally rise up into our first-floor space, so it was a passive solar system. We had also planned on installing a wind generator to supplement electricity, but there were too many height restrictions in place to allow a tower, so we let that idea go.

Each Step Gets Us Closer

Every step finished was a wonder to me as our dream became more tangible and defined. I wanted to have a very open design, but one that also allowed privacy. Our master bedroom was a good example of finding that balance. I wanted glass doors to the library loft to let in light, but that would also allow people in the living room to see into our bedroom. Offsetting the stairs and then building the river rock firewall solved the problem. To maintain the openness, I designed the oak stairs with treads that would be mortised in, so there wouldn't be any risers. Laying it all out and using my router on the stringers wasn't a problem, but assembling it all by myself was a major challenge. I decided to use two-part epoxy so I would have more time to fit all thirteen treads into place before it started setting up. I placed one stringer on a set of saw horses, mortises up, then I applied the epoxy and lined up the riser tenons — so far, so good. The hardest part was fitting the other stringer over all the treads at the same time! You simply can't do it without making adjustments and the longer you take, the more epoxy starts to drip out. I would love to see a video (without sound) of that procedure. Me running around, moving, squaring, and clamping everything in place with a couple dozen pipe clamps must have looked pretty funny. Extreme stress often transitions to extreme pleasure almost instantly in the case of building and furniture making. Once the assembly is completed, you can walk around and enjoy your creation. Mine looked like something between a 1940s attempt at atomic implosion and a set of Frankenstein twins. I couldn't wait until the next day when I could install it and see if my measurements and angles were correct. They were.

An invisible Rubicon is crossed at some point during a project of that magnitude — a point at which the seemingly endless steps in front of you shift, and you start to feel like an important corner was turned. Bringing in the drywallers was one of those corners. For months we had been able to look through our walls from one end of the house to the other. Now we couldn't. Everything took on a solid dimension, like rendering a computer drawing. I could no longer walk through the studs as a shortcut and without warning, both time and finish carpentry started accelerating. I customized our hickory cabinets and installed them in our baths and kitchen. We installed ceramic tile everywhere there wasn't carpet. All the components were coming together rapidly now. The drywall was taped and textured. Laura's brother, Mark, came out and sprayed our exterior and interior. I did all the finish trim work and installed our new wood stove and pipe which had been delivered the previous day. It was over 400 pounds and I was thankful to have the delivery guy help me set it in place on the stone hearth. The carpet was laid soon after that. I then assembled our walk-in closet organizers while listening to *Spirit* by Caroline Lavelle. To this day, every time I listen to that CD, I can smell new carpet and remember the unprecedented joy I felt as we approached the finish line.

It was on a Saturday afternoon, March 4, 2000, when it suddenly occurred to us that we could actually sleep there that night. Everything was done except receiving our CO (certificate of occupancy). We looked at each other and thought, let's do it! How can I express the emotions that coursed through me at the thought of our first night in our new home? One that we designed and built ourselves. As it happened, a fierce wind came up to shriek its celebration with us and we were so afraid of the large fixed windows being blown in from above that we spent our first evening reading up in the library loft, out of harm's way. Another constant reminder of this dream-made-real was coming off Highway 7 each day and turning right instead of left to our old rental place. Now we were coming home.

Chapter 24

I Need a Vacation

Now that our home was finished, we could get back to life as it was before. We were both exhausted from working every day for the last seven months. I continued to do furniture contracts out at the Y but there was also another element slowly rising to the surface in me that I wasn't even aware of for some time. We were both extremely relieved to have all that work behind us and because it had been at least two years since we had a vacation, we started planning a way to celebrate. Neither of us had ever been to Europe before, and as we started talking about where we would want to go, it surprised us to discover that we both chose the same destination for our first time going across the Pond. Even though we were already living in the mountains, we both wanted to go to Switzerland more than any other place. We knew that it would be different from Colorado, but we didn't realize just how much. We still have a running joke about what we call glaciers here. Perhaps Laura took it a little personally as a Colorado native, but I could never again call anything in the park a true glacier after seeing the real thing in Switzerland. What we had here were permanent snowfields to me.

Even more than the activity and size of the glaciers, what surprised me the most was how lush and green the country was. And manicured! Every property and field looked like a well-tended golf course. The architecture was magnificent and every bit as romantic as the pictures suggest. We landed in Zürich after a fourteen-hour flight and I spent my first fifteen minutes in that beautiful country bent over a toilet in the airport bathroom trying to decide whether or not to throw up. Air travel doesn't bother me but going without sleep can tend to make me nauseous. I really was right on the verge of losing it but became absolutely determined not to have that be my first experience overseas. I willed myself not to spill the beans and stood up and joined Laura, probably looking as white as Johnny and Edgar Winter combined. I still wasn't feeling that great but it's amazing what you can overcome if you just decide to. I had sat next to a Swiss high-school boy named Andre on the flight and a friendship had quickly grown between us. He was kind enough to show us around the airport and get us on the right train to Interlaken, which was another two hours from the airport. The three of us stood there before boarding, a little awkward and reluctant to ask for each other's contact information. That we didn't became a deep regret later as he had told us he would be in Interlaken for several days finishing up school before going back to his hometown of Basel, and we had wanted to reconnect again.

My mind was dragging my stomach along like a drill sergeant with a new recruit, promising rest when we finally got to our reserved hotel room. Having to ride a train for two hours more was bad enough after our flight, but it was made even worse because I had to ride backward the whole way. Laura looked at me but knew better than to try to engage in meaningful conversation because I wasn't looking very chatty. I looked out the windows a little bit and saw some of the city scenery, but mostly I was just staring straight ahead, trying to hold down the mutiny that was threatening with every minute. We finally arrived at our hotel…after a cab ride(!) only to find out that our reserved room had been given away. There was a wedding party that decided to stay a little longer and so they had given them our room. The mutinous pirates in my stomach were now standing on the gunwales, waving their swords at my brain. How much more travel could I take?! Being very kind, they had already made arrangements for us in the nearby town of Wilderswil. This meant another cab ride up into the mountains. I didn't see anything on this unwelcome journey, and was barely cognizant as we checked in and dropped our bags in our room. Sleep!

A Better Switzerland

Four hours later, we awoke to a different world. Now, all the unspeakable charm began to overtake us as we looked more closely at our accommodations, which were rustic and woody in the best sense and scents. This was fantastic and far better than what we had reserved in Interlaken! We walked out our door and looked on the Swiss countryside for the first time. The green rolling hills before us were partially shrouded in tattered clouds, and there were (I'm not kidding) cows with bells scattered all around us, welcoming us to their own adventure with leisurely song. I suppose we could have started grazing beside them and they would've thought none the worse of us, but we had other fare in mind. We decided to walk into town and take in this unbelievable scenery as the sweet scent of a foreign landscape washed over us with every step. Instead of the noisy city environment of Interlaken, we were escorted by the gentle and contented munching of Swiss milk cows. How incredible is that? Often when our carefully organized plans are interrupted, it's because our Heavenly Father knows something greater that will please our hearts far more.

Smart

As we entered the streets of Wilderswil, one of the things we first noticed was a car not much longer than me if I lay down on the sidewalk beside it. This was our first sight of a Smart Car as originally made by the Swatch company. We also saw other cool models — many that we had never seen before, including one by Ford. I guess that was the first time I realized how customized marketing worked. How come we had never seen any of these cars in the United States? Most of our SUVs and trucks would've looked like a tank rolling into town during an occupation. I later found out that their clean diesel Smart Car got somewhere in the neighborhood of a 90 mpg equivalent. The petrol version was in the 60 mpg range. How could this be? Why did they have this available when we didn't? The answer is disturbingly easy: because we never demanded it. Manufacturers always had the technology, but were only too happy to cater to our loud demands for spaciousness and power, and to let us pay more reasonable prices at our pump. Fuel in Europe is very expensive and so they demand economy and smart, efficient design. We actually talked about trying to bring one of the Smart Cars over to America and then heard of other people who had attempted the same, but without success. One woman even bought a Smart Car and had it shipped over, but they refused to let it in at the docks, the reason being that they weren't "highway tested for safety" yet. As small as these cars were at just over eight feet long, they actually had one of the best crash safety reports out there, but that didn't seem to matter. It's my opinion American officials and manufacturers wouldn't allow the Smart Car in until they could somehow figure out a way to jam an eight-cylinder engine into it and reduce its fuel efficiency to 30 mpg. Ten years later, that's exactly what happened. Daimler-Benz bought the Smart Car, and by the time it was introduced to our marketplace, its fuel economy was down to between 30 and 40 mpg. This is so infuriating, but it's not my fight. We as a nation seem to be okay with it — wanting only more power instead of sensibility — and the oil companies are only too happy to oblige.

We soon found a restaurant and were thrilled to discover that they made homemade pizza. You would think that my stomach was still too tender for something like that, but pizza is the world's perfect food and good for everything that ails you. We had a wonderful meal and then looked around a little bit more before walking back up to our château. The next day we made our way back down to Interlaken and spent the day exploring that beautiful city. The majestic Alps and their (real) glaciers were absolutely breathtaking as a backdrop to the many parks in the center of town. I found a beautiful wristwatch in one small shop that cost me the outrageous amount of $40. They had several colors and I wish I had bought one of each, because I have never been able to find that brand again. Apparently, Swiss watchmakers are as numerous and common as T-shirt venders are in our resort towns.

Stalking Innocently

Thinking about our new friend, Andre, we wondered if there was any way of finding him. We knew he was in one of the high schools in town and decided we had nothing to lose by going to one of them and asking if they had a student by that name. We went to the front office of one school and told the story of how we met. She asked if we knew his last name, which we didn't, and then surprised us by turning the student ledger around so we could look through it to see if we found his info. Every high school student and all their personal contact information was right there in front of us. We really couldn't believe they were allowing us to look at this sensitive information. Can you imagine someone going into a high school here in the states and having that access? We didn't see his name, so we went to another high school and they did the exact same thing. Wow, this was unreal! We began to feel like stalkers even though we meant no harm. This was 2000 and the innocence and trust the principals of these schools exhibited, and how they responded to such requests, was astounding. It finally started to make Laura too uncomfortable at the thought of going to yet a third school, so we finally let it go and said goodbye to our friend.

One village that Laura had read about and wanted to visit was Grindelwald. We took the cog rail there and couldn't believe our eyes when we arrived. This small mountain village sat right at the base of the Eiger, with 10,000 feet of sheer granite rising above. Oh my goodness, we HAD to stay here! We found a charming place and went inside to the front desk. The couple in front of us were Americans and currently demanding that they be given a room facing the mountain. I could understand why they wanted that view, but we were both embarrassed by their obnoxious demeanor. As much as we wanted the same, I leaned over and whispered to Laura, "Let's just take whatever they give us and be grateful and pleasant." She understood and totally agreed. Our turn came up and we asked if they had a room for the night. They did and so we took it, just happy to be staying in this amazing place. We were on the third floor, but weren't sure what direction we would be facing. We opened the door and caught our breath. They had given us a corner room that not only faced the Eiger, but had two balconies! I don't know if they were so grateful that we didn't demand a view or they were just feeling generous, but we had to laugh out loud at the gift we were given without asking for it. We immediately went back down and reserved that same room for two more nights.

Mystery Light

We had such a spectacular view that it was hard to even want to go out and look around, but we did and found many delightful treasures in Grindelwald. Sometimes we would go out to the local market and buy fresh fruit, homemade bread and maybe some wine, and bring it back to our room so we could sit on the balcony(ies) and marvel at the sight before us. As the day faded into twilight, we noticed an orange light located about halfway up the vertical mountain side. What on earth could that be? For several nights we watched and pondered its significance and strange location. We finally went into a bookstore and perused several volumes before solving the mystery. Swiss engineers had blasted a rail tunnel through the very heart of the mountain that would take you to Kleine Scheidegg, where you could then take a gondola up to the highest point in Europe — the Jungfrau. Most people would stop at Kleine Scheidegg and have lunch outdoors as they gazed on the Alps above and around them. That destination is more than enough to deeply satisfy the soul. However, we wanted to go further up and experience the vistas from the height of Europe.

Climbing the Eiger is extremely dangerous because the face is rotten and is almost continually scoured by both rock and ice avalanches. They also have a notorious foehn wind there that can blast the mountainside and surrounding villages with hurricane-force power. To provide an escape route for mountaineers when conditions quickly erode, the Swiss have provided a small escape tunnel that connects with the rail tunnel so climbers can enter and walk back down. That light we had been seeing reveals where the wooden door to the escape tunnel is located on the cliff face. There's a story of a man who got caught climbing when the weather suddenly fell apart. He was able to locate the door and started walking down the tunnel when he saw a light ahead. This wasn't the light at the end of the tunnel we like to think of — this was a train coming up toward him. Swiss engineers take great pride in their precision. and so they only blasted the tunnel just wide enough to allow the train to pass through. The man obviously knew this and began to panic. How ironic to escape from the wall, and then get killed by the train. There was no time for him to race back to the auxiliary tunnel, so he had to find a small depression and hope he didn't get smeared along the wall like butter. He turned his head sideways and survived.

Flexibility

We realized this was an excellent way to travel: book one or two nights where you want to go and then leave the rest unscheduled so you can have the flexibility to stay longer or move on. We traveled to many other cities around the country, including an unscheduled and very brief trip to Italy. Laura remembered enough German from high school to keep us on track (pun intended) for the most part. On this occasion, our train to Lugano was about forty-five minutes out and we saw that there was another one leaving in ten minutes, so we quickly decided to catch that one. This train seemed a little different than what we had experienced before; it was more luxurious and completely empty. That was enough to unsettle us, but we could only continue and hope for the best. The truth came when the conductor arrived to inspect our passes. I instantly think of the *Polar Express* now, when the little girl didn't have her ticket. This was far worse because the conductor didn't speak English or German — and he certainly didn't have the charm of Tom Hanks. He indicated that he wanted our passports, so we handed them over and then watched in horror as he opened the window and pretended to throw them out. It was very clear that we were on the wrong train and we didn't know where we were going or what would become of us. We finally understood that we were going to Milan, and didn't have the rail passes to be on that train. We stopped in a small town in Italy and he communicated that we had to get off. We felt like we were about to be lined up and shot as he pointed across an empty field. We saw a bus on the other side and wondered if we were supposed to get on that. He seemed to think so, and though we didn't know if that was correct or even where it was going, we decided we had better try. We climbed on and it turned out to be the right decision — the bus took us back across the border into Switzerland. By the time we got back to our destination, it was late and we realized we hadn't eaten in eight hours and now all the restaurants were closed. We found a vending machine and bought four-dollar cokes and a large box of Swiss candy called Toffifay, and that was our dinner. We later found the same delicious candy in Safeway in Estes and relived our adventurous day and night in Italy and Switzerland.

Chapter 25

The Velvet Hammer

Technology never stops advancing, and musical equipment is no exception. My Akai 16-track unit I recorded my first CD, *The Good Life*, with was already outdated in the two years it took us to design and build our home. Fortunately, 24-bit computer-based recording was now available and at a much lower price than Pro Tools offered. I basically had to start all over again and buy new equipment, but at least computers allowed you to upgrade and be modular. Anyone who works with computers for a living understands that this is both a blessing and a curse. The more programs you own, the more you have to deal with compatibility issues every time someone releases a software update. All the same, it was a huge benefit to move onto that platform because it allowed automation of my faders and other mixing parameters. If you were doing all that with a mouse, it could be pretty cumbersome, but control surfaces were just around the corner. There was a program I wanted that was only available on Windows OS so I decided to switch and had a music company called Sound Chasers build me a system specifically tuned for recording. In the year 2000, computers were still finicky enough that you had to pay close attention to all the components and how they worked together for audio, with hard drive speeds and throughput at the top of the list. I bought Steinberg's Nuendo 2 as my recording software and WaveLab for editing, along with GigaStudio for virtual instruments, and entered a major learning curve that would last for some time.

In the pleasure and afterglow of finishing our home, I didn't realize that something else was happening inside me that was draining my energy. I thought I was still recovering from all the stress and physical labor involved over the last two years, and I'm sure that's true, but I think I was also becoming a little depressed and that's the part I couldn't figure out. I had just accomplished something I never thought could actually happen; how could I be feeling down? It wasn't until several years later that I heard about the emotional letdown people experience after accomplishing a goal. I never would have guessed that condition even existed, except I was experiencing it without knowing the cause. I know it sounds strange to say this, but I think the fact that I was now settled into one permanent place had a role in it as well. Moving eleven times in a two-year period is a royal pain, but it also provides stimulation from the sense of adventure and constant change. That can become addictive without you even realizing it. You see it a lot more often in those personalities who move from one relationship to another just to keep the initial thrill alive, but I would never have anticipated that same element from renting! I think I was also starting to feel the effects of being isolated after being around the vibrant community at the YMCA for nine years. The furniture contracts lasted anywhere from one to three months, and as I did the work back in my old woodshop on the Y grounds, that provided me with some temporary social activities. But even that felt different now that I was no longer working there full time. You don't want it to happen, but it seems inevitable that a very slow separation starts occurring between you and those you worked with for so long. In a paradoxical (but still tangible) sense, you and they have moved on, even if no one has changed locations. There's a common bond and mutual purpose that's lost, and though friendships can certainly survive beyond that virtual separation, it's never exactly the same, either.

Subtle Changes

There was also something deeper at issue with my soul that I still couldn't see, or at least acknowledge yet. When you're driving toward a large city, you can subtly start to feel yourself becoming tense and nervous even though you're still thirty miles out. That's because other roads and highways are beginning to merge more frequently and the traffic around you is slowly increasing and you are only aware of these changes on a subconscious level. Sometimes I experience that same subconscious awareness in my life. Several roads are converging and I don't know what's coming toward me, but something is approaching.

On November 13, I went down to Boulder to help my father-in-law put Christmas lights up on his two-story house. He had built it himself and used wood shake shingles which were thicker than what you could buy now. As a result, they lasted far beyond the average life expectancy, but they were also very dry and brittle by this time. It had snowed earlier in the month and even though there was none on the roof now, it was still very cold so I wore my hiking boots to provide extra traction and to keep my feet warm. We were walking around hanging lights from the second story fascia, when I remembered that I had some candy in my pocket that I wanted to give to my mother-in-law, Ann, who was hanging lights from the ground. I called to her and started walking toward the edge to throw the candy down…

I woke up on the sidewalk.

I had no idea what had happened or why I was on the ground. Gary and Ann were both beside me and trying to decide whether to call an ambulance or not. I was pretty fuzzy but able to communicate reasonably well and told them I thought I was okay but that my right wrist hurt a little bit. The more they talked to me the more worried they became, and decided to drive me to the hospital themselves. This was a good decision. By the time we got to the front entrance, I was completely loopy and fading fast. I remember being in a wheelchair as they pushed me toward the ER while asking me questions about the date, my name, and who was president. Laura arrived at that moment and they asked me if I recognized her. I said yes, she was my wife. Then they asked me if I knew her name. Okay, this was a puzzler. I thought that I had a pretty good chance of getting it right — eventually. And here's one of the very few times I've been impressed by myself. I still had enough smarts up there to say, "I think so, but I'd rather not guess." That's pretty clever for a guy who just fell on his head! Laura is the most understanding person in the world, but what would she think if I named six other women before getting it right?

This is what I think happened: the snow that had fallen a week before melted and was absorbed by the dry wood shingles. The temperature was below zero overnight and the water froze. I couldn't see any difference and I must have stepped on one, slipped and fallen back hard enough to knock myself unconscious, and then slid off the roof like a one-man toboggan. I dimly remember trying to grab at the rain gutter with my right hand as I went over the edge. What difference this made in my position and trajectory is a complete mystery to me. It's extremely humbling to realize that I fell ten feet onto concrete with absolutely no control in how I landed. I had a three-inch skull fracture and a broken right wrist. The nurses discovered the wrist injury as they tried to jam an IV into it. I don't remember any of that experience but I was told that I briefly revisited my "Angry Builder" phase and told them exactly what I thought of their attempt to insert a sharp object into my injured wrist.

Not-So-Subtle Changes

I faded in and out but eventually woke up in the ICU around nine-thirty at night, wired up like a circuit board and sweating like a pig. I immediately realized that I had slept all day due to the head injury and morphine and was now looking at a night of being wide awake, immobile, and slowly roasted alive. I panicked at that moment and actually became claustrophobic for the next year. I had never been bothered by tight spaces, but the thought of being miserably hot and constrained pushed me right over the edge. I don't know what the temperature was in that room but it felt like walking into a nursing home where they keep it swelteringly hot. I complained and my nurse took pity on me and turned off the nuclear reactor nearby. Even though I had been out of my unheated cabin for five years now, my metabolism was still royally screwed up. Moving into Estes Park and a normal house had been like dropping an Eskimo off in Florida. Good luck! See ya!

My caregivers were excellent and they did everything possible to make me comfortable. I was monitored overnight to see if the pressure on my brain would require surgery and then was moved into a private room for two more days. Even though the heat was turned off, I was still uncomfortably warm and so they started opening the window for me. It was really funny to wake up and see that I had visitors who were all wearing heavy coats and gloves. It must have been freezing in there, but that was the only way I could be relatively comfortable. Even though I was still on morphine, I had a headache that never went away during those three days. It was finally determined I would not need surgery and I could go home after they put a cast on my wrist. My last day in the hospital was when I made a startling discovery: I couldn't taste my food — at all! For most people, not tasting hospital food might be seen as a good thing. For someone with a head injury, this is not good news because it might not come back. Even a cotton ball soaked with ammonia and held right under my nose didn't register anything. Having 100-percent loss of taste and smell is a strange sensation, and is a condition which leaves doctors without room for an accurate prognosis. It might come back, it might not. There's just no way to tell until it happens (or not), and that could take up to a year.

To read about that condition probably sounds worse than it was actually experiencing it. It wasn't nearly as depressing as it seems like it would be, and created in me a novel curiosity about it more than anything else. It also revealed interesting psychological and sociological effects as

Laura began trying to feed me things that I wouldn't eat before, such as cheese. The problem (for her) was that I still had my memory and I remembered what it smelled like before — stinky feet in the case of Parmesan. One good thing that came out of it was I stopped drinking diet Dr Pepper. I had gotten to where I was drinking five or six cans a day. I figured that since I couldn't taste it, I might as well switch to seltzer because the carbonation was the only sensation I could detect and enjoy. I had another headache for two weeks after I stopped drinking the DPs, which tells you something.

Warped Perceptions

It was wonderful to be home again, but the stairs up to our bedroom presented problems. Laura would have to help me climb them and then put me into bed because my balance was so messed up. I would violently shiver every night for several minutes as I adjusted both to the temperature and horizontal position. The next morning, she would have to help me to get up and back down the stairs before leaving for work. Her tender care for me during this time was amazing. I would have food, drink, and anything else I might possibly need during the day right there beside me. Light became an issue for me because of the lingering effects of claustrophobia, and I would begin to experience dread as the afternoon leaned into twilight and then darkness. My little circle of light became my world, and a small world it was. We started keeping every light on around me to help alleviate the sensation of the world closing in on me. For the next year, I had a hard time being in the middle of a dense crowd because I needed to know that I could move if I wanted to. Even being in the middle of a row in a movie theater could bring me near the edge of panic. If someone had come up from behind and put their arms around me during that first year, I very well might have come out swinging. I'm not a violent person but I could have become one during that period. Unless you have experienced it, it's impossible to convey how much a head injury affects your life, including your perception of everything around you. I would rather have an injury anywhere else on my body than my head; that *really* messes with you.

If you'll pardon the pun, trephination isn't all it's cracked up to be. The idea of drilling a hole through your skull so your brain can get more oxygen is hideously primitive and ignorant. On the other hand, I did experience heightened sensations and emotions over the next couple of years as my injured brain repaired itself. The best news came as I started to smell again after several months. It was very subtle and unpredictable at first. The really odd thing was that it didn't come back as a whole with each component intact and in balance, like raising the volume knob on your stereo would be. This was more like sitting in front of the original studio mixer and raising certain faders — but not others. Random individual contributors to the overall scent came through but others were filtered out, leaving me with a strange, but not unwelcome insight into the composition of what scent really is. You can build any sound in the world using a combination of pure sine waves, but if you remove seventy percent of them, what you have left sounds very different from the original. This is what I was experiencing with increasing intensity over the next several years. More and more of those faders were being raised now, but it still wasn't a completed scent. Another strange twist was that one or two of those faders would often remain raised for a long time after the others faded into silence.

Our good friends, Katy and Ole, were concerned about me and offered to help in whatever way they could. Ole came over one day and carried a far more comfortable chair down from upstairs for me to enjoy. Katy came over to just sit and talk on one memorable day. The sun was out and she was wearing a cheerful yellow sweater — and unknowingly created an indelible impression, one which stayed with me long after she left — to help ward off the encroaching darkness each night. Laura's parents bought an air mattress that we could keep in the living room so I wouldn't have to navigate the stairs every night. My sister, Lee Ann, was a nurse and she came over often and took excellent care of me as well. It was a very slow process, but I was starting to feel normal again; and as Laura's birthday started drawing near, I decided on a present for her. I wrote and recorded a song ("Laura's Song") to show my appreciation for the outstanding care she had given me, and surprised her with it on her birthday. When you play your own original composition and someone cries, you hope it isn't because it's so bad. I think she really liked it.

True Humility

During my recovery, I began to think back and replay what had happened on that day, and realized how far differently things could have turned out. I was unconscious when I fell and could easily have landed directly on my head, killing me instantly. Or I could have broken my neck or my back. A hundred different complications could have resulted from that fall — some permanently. What difference did it make when I grabbed at the rain gutter? How did that action change my original orientation relative to how I hit the ground? All these questions began to haunt me and I clearly understood how precarious my position was. I thought about how distant I had become in my relationship to Christ, and how easily He could have taken me on that day. I believed that I would have still gone to Heaven, even with my lukewarm attitude, but I also knew that wasn't the state in which I wanted to enter eternity. True humility and gratitude began to overwhelm me as I thought about the Lord doing whatever it takes to draw us back to Him. Does that sound cruel to you? That God loves us enough to get our attention by whatever means necessary? Not if you truly believe what He says about being the only source of life and the unimaginable consequences of rejecting that. You wouldn't hesitate to push your child out of the way of a speeding car, even while knowing that they might break a bone, if it meant saving their life. The thought of God allowing or even causing distress or pain in order to save us from a far worse fate is almost unthinkable in our pampered American society. That's because most people don't honestly believe in "a far worse fate" (i.e., hell). If they did, they would be grateful for the intervention.

There's no way to prove that God was directly involved in my fall, but given my past history and the retroactively clear evidence of what happened when I didn't heed past warnings, I have no trouble attributing it to Him, or at least the good result of it. To me, it felt like God's velvet hammer: a way to clearly get my attention without causing irreparable harm. I think I'm at least as good as I ever was (don't go there), so it was a welcome event. If that's what it took to draw my heart back to His after ten years, then I'm grateful.

Chapter 26

Momentum

Momentum can be your friend or it can be your enemy, depending on which direction it's moving you.

In the same way that nothing in the universe is ever truly static or motionless, humans are always in motion as well. We are either ascending or descending; moving toward or away from that place in which we are happiest and healthiest in mind, body, and spirit. If you are honest with yourself, you can usually tell which way you are going at any given moment. I know perfectly well when I'm making choices and developing patterns that aren't good for me, but recognizing it and doing something about it are entirely different things. Momentum naturally builds on itself and you have to either nurture it if it's good (keep it going), or find a way to arrest the motion if it's bad. I'm fully aware of those times when I am gaining weight because of poor eating habits, but I don't care enough to halt or change it until I reach some point of disgust or criticality, and then it's a long haul to get back to where I want to be through dieting. It would be much better and wiser to weigh myself once or twice a week and deal with a couple of pounds rather than wait until I have to lose twenty or more. If only we could look into a mirror or step on a scale to clearly see where we are spiritually, and make a change before we stray too far. For you see, the farther you stray and longer you stay there, the less you can discern that you are even off course. Men (especially) are notoriously bad at asking for help when they know they're lost. Try giving directions to one who doesn't even think he is. Apparently, it was beyond my ability to stop my subtle descent, and it took divine intervention to help me break that harmful cycle I was in. My newly tenderized heart was now turned toward God and receptive in a way that it hadn't been for many years, and I could feel life slowly pouring into me again.

Back to the (Musical) Bars

It had now been six years since I recorded *The Good Life* in 1997. I had set aside music in order to build our home and my studio, and now it was time to take it up again. Even though I loved the variety it provided, changing hats from builder/woodworker to musician didn't happen instantly. It took some time to shift mentally and emotionally and get into a creative groove again — especially after the two years I had been away this time. Sometimes it would take a couple weeks just to let my hands heal enough to play guitar after all the splinters, cuts, and normal wear and tear from working on my continuing furniture contracts. Writing and recording "Laura's Song" started the good momentum that I needed to make my next album, *World of Colors*. I was enjoying a new sophistication in writing style, and the technological opportunities with my new computer setup were vastly superior to what I had used before. It made me feel like I had been building a ship in a bottle with *The Good Life*, and now I was building one to scale — one that I could actually walk around in. The contrast was that strong and liberating.

I was very pleased with how *World of Colors* sounded and it was so nice to take my time with the production and mastering process. I sent it off to the replication house, booked another show at Summerfest, and began remixing my new material so I could perform it live. I had bought a Parker Midifly electric and could now play many of the sounds and parts that I had recorded; in fact, most of the instrumentation was played from my new guitar, including the drums on "Night-Scented Flowers". It's kind of ironic that I can't play some of my piano performances on piano! If I originally composed and triggered it from my guitar, I'm not good enough to transfer it over easily because of the finger positions and voicing unique to each instrument. On the plus side, I could now play anything I wanted with this new setup and change on the fly (pun intended). For example, on one song I might start with an acoustic sound provided by my Piezo bridge pickup, switch to a cathedral organ, throw in a few hammered dulcimer arpeggios and then solo with a Mesa Boogie amp simulation. Trying to be cutting edge is pretty darn expensive, though! Not only did I have to rebuild my recording equipment from the ground up, I also had to buy all-new gear to perform live, which included a Dell Inspiron laptop and a second copy of Nuendo ($$$!) to enable me to play all these different sounds. I was doing this way before it became popular and had to be very creative in finding solutions and work-arounds to use all this equipment in my live performances because no one wrote programs with this purpose in mind yet.

Work-Arounds

I wanted to use the automation feature in Nuendo to

change my sounds for me so I could concentrate on playing instead. To do this, I had to set up a separate project for each song I played live, then create stereo tracks for my accompaniment and another stereo track for my live guitar processing. For I not only played sampled instruments from my guitar, I also used the mastering effects in the program, like chorus, delay etc. I know it's hard for people to believe this now, but I was using a (single!) lowly Pentium III processor to do all this live input processing with a single 5,400 rpm drive, and it could keep up without a hiccup. I had to install a second 7,500 rpm drive for all my sampled instruments, which meant that I had to sacrifice my optical drive space. This was a royal pain whenever I needed to install more software. I also created separate partitions on my OS drive so I could tweak it specifically for audio use. Simply writing about all this wears me out now! I can't believe I did so much just to use it in this way. But in addition to the sheer fun of playing with this kind of versatility and creativity, I also hoped this would help set me apart from the other tens of thousands who were also taking advantage of independent recording. This is another instance when it would have helped to be better at marketing myself and drawing attention to what I was doing. The general public usually doesn't notice those kinds of things without explanation, which I quickly started doing at almost every show. The people responsible for hiring entertainment usually don't care, as I found out much to my chagrin. A lot of them don't have any musical knowledge in the first place and don't know or appreciate the difference between someone strumming a thirty-dollar acoustic and someone like myself who's spent several thousand to provide something more unique for the audience.

Remixing my songs allowed me to drop out all the fun parts and play them live, and Nuendo would switch sounds automatically. There were some songs where I played along with my backing tracks and then they would stop while I played on live for anywhere from several seconds to a whole minute before they rejoined me. This created a problem because my timing had to be perfect — impossible for anything longer than about ten seconds. I finally found a command hidden within a menu called "Play To Next Marker." This would work! I could split the audio file at the point where I began playing solo, move the new section a little to the right in the timeline and place a marker right at the beginning of it. The playback would reach the marker and pause, waiting for me to hit a footswitch right when I needed it to start playing with me again. A lot of programming and trouble, but it was worth it once I got everything set up. The only hassle was having to close each song and open the next one.

Another thing that changed while I was building my home was that secular musicians had discovered churches to be a very lucrative market and started playing there while pretending to be Christians. Say an "Amen!" or "Praise the Lawd!" or other expected church-speak, and you were in like Flynn, selling CDs and making hundreds or even thousands of dollars a pop. Of course, they started targeting megachurches exclusively because of the large audience and potential $$$. I had no idea this was going on and became frustrated and discouraged when no one ever called me back even after I left multiple messages. What was going on?? It wasn't until many months later that I found out the truth from a worship pastor who was also a friend. He said that he received close to one hundred calls and emails a week from bands traveling around the country asking to come play at their church. These trusting pastors finally realized they were being bamboozled and taken advantage of and stopped allowing outside musicians to come play in their churches altogether. Another case of a few ruining it for the many (or possibly the many ruining it for the few). I loved playing at churches and sharing both my music and testimony of how He had awakened my heart after so long. That opportunity was now taken from me and other true believers because of greed.

Honored

Two very encouraging events happened that same year, though. The owner of CD Baby, Derek Sivers, wrote to inform me that they had chosen *World of Colors* as their Album of the Month. This was the biggest independent distributor in the world! They gave me an incredible review and posted it on their homepage for millions of people to see. That was one fabulous December and Christmas, I can tell you! The other blessing happened when a couple came to see a show, bought my CDs and then called the next day to ask me to meet them at the YMCA Rustic Cafe. Duane and Connie Cooper lived in Spring, Texas (a suburb of Houston), loved my music, and wanted me to come play at their church and stay with them. I was thrilled by the invitation, bought my airline tickets, and made arrangements for transporting my equipment. Duane met me at Bush International and drove me back to their beautiful home after first showing me where I would be playing the next morning. This wasn't some small country church — this was Cypress Creek Community Center, a beautiful and large facility that held all kinds of community events throughout the year. I was a little intimidated by the sight, but my nerves were more than soothed by my new friends and their incredible hospitality. The next morning dawned and the worship team welcomed me into their midst with total warmth and genuine excitement. That further placed me at ease and I began to relax as I prepared to perform special music for the contemporary service. Everything went very well and the congregation responded so beautifully, it felt like I had been playing for seven hundred close friends. Duane and Connie, showed me around Spring that afternoon and overwhelmed me with their down-home charm. On the way to the airport the next day, Duane talked about his beautiful wife and revealed she was an actor who worked with many Hollywood stars like Kevin Costner, Glenn Close, and others of their fame and stature. I would never have guessed! Connie was so humble and fun, and talked about everything except her amazing career. There was one other thing on my mind as we drove on and I asked him about it. In many rooms of their home, I had noticed an identical picture of a hauntingly beautiful young woman and it began to trouble my heart, wondering if she was their daughter and fearing the story behind that image.

I finally asked him and he told me that the picture was of Lauren, their nineteen-year-old daughter, and that she had been hit head-on by a drunk driver and killed instantly while driving with friends on a ski trip. My heart crumbled as I realized that my suspicion was correct. I can't even begin to imagine the pain they or anyone else would have to endure after losing a child. As an outsider, you always feel so helpless because you want to do something to express your sorrow and share their pain in some small way, even if from the great distance of experience and time. During the two-hour flight back to Denver, I started thinking about Lauren and what she had experienced seconds after that horrific crash, and how different her parents' mourning would be if they could see the breathtaking splendor and bliss she was surrounded by and filled with now. Lauren was more alive than she had ever been here on earth; her tears and pain forever left behind as she looked upon the face of Christ. However, on this side of eternity, the loss and anger is often overwhelming as we are left with only the mortal remains and the often traumatic manner in which someone died. Letting go of the last images and details has to be the hardest part in the long process of healing; it certainly was for my family as we watched helplessly as the ravages of cancer destroyed my mother's body. The gift of feeling her presence and well-being that afternoon back in 1984 had set my heart free, knowing she was no longer in that body but feeling His life and joy as we were always meant to. Even the most peaceful death is absolutely tragic because it's death — something none of us were ever intended to experience.

"In My Father's Arms"

When I got home, I gave the only gift I had to offer — a song in Lauren's honor. In some ways, it's harder to capture emotions through instrumental music because people relate to words so much more easily. On the other hand, music has the ability to bypass language altogether and resonate directly with someone's soul. I wanted the pure timbre of a grand piano and chose to write a solo piece without any accompaniment. I composed it on my Parker Midifly and triggered a Steinway grand. I told my wife, Laura, that I had written a new song and played it for her when she got home that night. She really didn't know what to expect, but began weeping a few seconds into the song. That set my own tears flowing as I saw how it affected her and as I imagined presenting the song to Lauren's parents. A few weeks later, I told Duane that I had composed a song and called it "In My Father's Arms." He was deeply touched and asked me if I would come back sometime soon and perform it live for Connie and their church family. It would be a complete surprise; no one would know what I was going to play except Duane. I was so happy to do that for this wonderful couple and to see my other new friends again, so we made all the arrangements for my return.

To be honest, I don't know how my new song was introduced or by whom, because I was distracted in my preparation. I think it might have been Duane who introduced the song. As I began, Connie began weeping and I prayed that God Himself would use this music to help cleanse and heal one of the deepest wounds known on earth: a mother's grief over the loss of her child.

I had a very hard time myself trying to keep my composure as I played, imagining what Connie was feeling. Then I started noticing something that was a welcome distraction and made me smile inside. The whole band had left the stage when it was time for me to play that song, so I was up there standing alone with my electric guitar. As I looked out on the congregation, I noticed that many people were looking at me, then over at the grand piano on stage, and then back at me again. This confused me at first until I understood their confusion. They were hearing the sound of a grand piano and there was no one on stage except me and my guitar! They could see that I was playing this solo piece, but where was that sound coming from? At one point, I almost laughed out loud as

I looked at their confounded expressions. That whole experience was a very special one for all of us, including the many who had walked with this precious couple through one of the darkest times they could imagine. I would make many more trips to Cypress Creek and always stayed with the Coopers, soaking up their gracious ways. The only awkward time that occurred between us was when we ordered out for pizza and Duane and I watched a college football game between my favorite Texas Longhorns and his alma mater, Texas A&M. He was very passionate about his team and I did my very best not to rub it in as my Longhorns royally cleaned their clocks! I'm just grateful he didn't make me take a taxi back to the airport the next morning.

Songs of Faith

Writing "In My Father's Arms" inspired me to work on my next CD, *Forgiven*. I usually avoided titles of faith because I wanted my music to reach everyone, instead of being dismissed as "religious music" (which is pretty funny because it's instrumental, so it shouldn't matter). That actually happened, though, when I later gave a copy to a guy who worked at Domino's Pizza. I saw him again a couple weeks later and asked how he liked the album, to which he sheepishly admitted that he hadn't listened to it at all, but gave it to his brother instead. I pointed out that my music was instrumental, but that didn't seem to make any difference — he didn't want anything to do with it because of a bad encounter with Christians earlier in his life. Oh, well…

I really enjoyed the recording process on this album because I had once again updated my equipment and software, resulting in the cleanest production quality I had yet achieved, in my opinion. I started the CD off with a two-minute cathedral organ, beautifully sampled inside Notre Dame in Budapest. This gave way to a rocking rendition of "When I Survey the Wondrous Cross," which I played in both sound and style as a tribute to Eric Johnson. I was very pleased with this album, but I never took my own advice about nurturing momentum. I should have kept writing after each CD, because you get into a very efficient creative groove, but I would always stop and focus on performing and promoting my newest release instead. I played the title cut, "Forgiven," at a men's retreat in Estes Park and totally screwed it up. It's a very difficult song technically and my coordination just wasn't up to it that night. I was heading back to Cypress Creek again the next week and I had to decide whether to play that song or not as part of my setlist. Everything inside me screamed, "NO!" because of that last experience. Feeling humiliated in front of one hundred men was bad enough; what would it feel like in front of seven hundred? For some reason, I still felt confident enough to go ahead and perform it.

This was the only trip I made down there in the month of December, and it ended up being the most memorable one. Their beautiful home and neighborhood was all-out decorated for Christmas and I walked around in the evenings feeling like I was in some sort of wonderful dream. Believe it or not, I chose to perform "Forgiven" first, out of the four songs I played. Nothing like running out of the gate! Against all odds, I played it flawlessly and received a standing ovation. They gave me an identical response for each song I played, as if they thought this was my last time there. It actually would be my last time, but I certainly didn't know that, nor did they. All performers know of at least one transcendental moment during their careers, and for me this was one that would stand alone among others. To play in front of so many sweet, generous people and not feel the least hint of nervousness; to feel connected, understood, and appreciated like I did that morning is a once-in-a-lifetime experience I will never forget. Thank you Duane, Connie, and my friends at Cypress Creek, for changing a part of me forever.

Chapter 27

The Unthinkable

Back in 1997, after releasing *The Good Life*, I had played "Snowfall in Vienna" at First Baptist Church in Estes Park. Everyone there was very nice but one man in particular stood apart as he came up to introduce himself and express his appreciation for my being there and sharing my gift. His name was Mark Roskam and there seemed to be an instant connection between us. Over the years, we saw each other occasionally around town and there was always a strong affinity for each other, but it never went beyond a brief encounter into actual friendship. I remember once at a restaurant, where he literally jumped out of his seat and ran across to say hello when he saw me. That kind of outward warmth and affection is rare in a man, and I have always respected that character trait and see it in other men as a sign of security and strength in their masculinity. It shocked me the first time I saw my father-in-law kiss his two sons on the lips. Here was a "manly-man" superintendent for one of the largest building contractors in America, telling two strapping six-footers that he loved them and then planting a big one on their ruby reds! And they were all so comfortable with it — that was the other thing that surprised me. I was more familiar with the fathers who would say, "I've never actually told my kids I love them, but they know it." Growing up without a father myself, I guess I never gave it that much thought, but seeing it expressed so freely definitely made a big impact on me. I'll never forget when Gary was going into surgery and we were all standing around his bed praying for him. One by one, he said goodbye and kissed the rest of them. I was shaking his hand when he suddenly pulled me down and kissed me right on the lips. I didn't know whether to wipe my mouth immediately or ask him out on a date! Wow, I sure wasn't used to that freedom of affection between men, but my respect for this man and his family grew exponentially that day.

Lasting Friendship

Mark Roskam never kissed me (don't try it, buster!) but his ability to let his guard down and be vulnerable was an undeniable strength and indication of his character. Maybe growing up with three women allowed me to become fully comfortable with showing my affection and articulating my thoughts, but I could easily relate to and talk with this guy. I've never been one who went to a party with a date and then immediately sequestered myself with the other men in another room with a great sigh of relief. I feel equally comfortable with both sexes, but often find myself talking to women because they usually have the ability to express their thoughts and emotions more easily than most men. Regardless of gender, I love it when I find someone who can just as easily be excited by a subject as I am, and enjoy it without becoming self-conscious. Mark was one of those rare men who could do that, and after five years of two-minute conversations, we finally decided to make a real friendship out of it and began spending time together. He was the associate pastor of First Baptist in

Estes Park and certainly had a strong interest in bringing people together in fellowship; however, he was sensitive and wise enough not to try to push me in that direction. It had been twelve years now since I had been actively involved in any church and I wasn't the least bit interested in returning to that environment anytime soon. If he had pushed, I think I would have backed away from our friendship. Fortunately, he didn't, and we were able to enjoy each other's company and even talk about God, but without any pressure or expectations. That's wisdom.

Something that came out of our conversations regarding his history really surprised me. I found myself running to his side in defense as I heard about some injustices he had suffered. Where was I when all this was going on? Why wasn't I there to stand beside him and speak up on his behalf? I began to feel that I had been inactive on the sideline while wars were raging all around me. It's very interesting to see how God navigates around our carefully laid-out barriers and defenses. C. S. Lewis laid his finger on it when he said, "a young man who wishes to remain a sound atheist cannot be too careful of his reading. There are traps everywhere — 'Bibles laid open, millions of surprises,' as Herbert says, 'fine nets and stratagems.' God is, if I may say it, very unscrupulous" (Lewis, *Joy, 262*).

I love that quote! I love Lewis' honesty and clarity about what most of us feel but are afraid or unable to say. It seems that He was at work again here; igniting a protectiveness on behalf of my new friend, in order to begin a new motivation that superseded all my other objections. It shared certain elements with the emotion that I felt when I wasn't in touch with my childhood friend, Steve, and lost him without being able to say goodbye. We are no match for God, and His creativity knows no bounds as He relentlessly pursues a deeper relationship with each one of us. I can clearly remember that day in 2002 as Mark and I talked in my living room when a sleeping giant awakened within me.

Have Hope, All Ye Who Enter Here

Like many people, I live within a dichotomy. I can be alone and be very happy and contented. I also love being around people as well. What I couldn't recognize was how much I missed and suffered from being outside of fellowship with other believers. I didn't think I missed it at all and had been happy riding my bike and hiking on weekends. I still enjoyed my relationship to Christ, so why did I need to go to church? That's where I was in 2002. I had no interest in pursuing church membership or even attending regularly, but I still wanted to share whatever musical talent God had given me with the people in those churches. Mark was now employed at Rocky Mountain Church and our friendship provided the vital connection to their worship pastor, Chris Moody. Together, they made arrangements for me to come and play special music in all three services without even auditioning me first. That in itself was incredibly gracious. I chose to perform "Laura's Song" for some inexplicable reason. Maybe the steel drums warmed everyone's heart that cold November 2 evening in 2002. Whatever the reason, the people at Rocky Mountain E-Free Church responded very enthusiastically and I remember the lead pastor, Jess Mahon, turning toward me during the last service, thanking me and saying that I was welcome to come back and play anytime. That really meant a lot to me and I determined at that moment that I would indeed return very soon. Of course, I had to go and look up "E-Free" to see what the heck that meant! I was relieved to discover that it stood for evangelical free, which simply meant it was congregationally ruled instead of by deacons or elders. Okay, I felt better.

A few weeks later, I came to perform again and this time I was able to relax and pay more attention to my surroundings since I had already been there once before. I started noticing how different these people were; there was none of that country-club atmosphere that I rebelled against. These people were very down to earth and sincerely cared for each other in a natural and unpretentious way. I was also deeply impressed by the leadership and how they related to the congregation. They didn't just talk about what rascals they used to be in their former life; they talked honestly about the issues they struggled with right then! That really got my attention and I found it extremely refreshing. Once again, something remarkable was sneaking through my defenses against my will. Laura and I had already tried to reenter that world by visiting the Methodist church in Estes several times, but without success. I quickly stopped going and she only went a few more times before stopping herself. Laura had gone with me each time I played at Rocky Mountain and was also enjoying the experience, so we kept going back each Sunday. We talked about visiting other churches in town, but when each Sunday morning came around, we always felt drawn back there again. Pretty soon, we gave up the pretense of trying other churches and attended Rocky Mountain every week.

One Sunday morning, Chris asked me if I would like to join the worship team. I really liked the musicians there a lot and said I'd think about it. Inside, I was still resisting that kind of commitment to anything related to church, but especially with music because I felt it was so inferior to everything secular that I listened to. However, the high level of musicianship in this band and their engaging personalities were steadily eroding that resolve. I finally made the decision to join them and found it far less painful than I imagined. None of the songs were difficult at all but it was still hard to learn so many since I had never heard any of them before. I had to have lead sheets at first, but I quickly decided that I wanted to memorize all of them and be free to look out at the congregation instead. It was a relief after a few weeks when we started repeating ones that I already knew. Several of the others in the band were very familiar with all my favorite groups and loved them just as much as I did. I hadn't encountered this before and again, found it so refreshing. This group wasn't "churchy" like I had experienced before; these people were just like me — very aware and appreciative of the good things "outside" of church.

The result was that I truly let down my guards and started to come to life in a way that astounded me. I went to one of Mark Roskam's classes and started asking troubling questions. Instead of getting me kicked out, it ended up impressing them and resulted in my being asked to join several boards, such as Adult Education and Creative Arts — which I accepted. This was crazy! A few months ago, I wasn't interested in being anywhere near a church as far as involvement as concerned, yet here I was, getting more and more involved and excited each week. This was good, and surprisingly fun, but I recognized that I was still carrying several pounds of tasty rebellion around with me. Hmm, what to do with that? I became newly fascinated with the Bible and wanted to dig deeper and deeper into the original languages so I could better understand it — I even started teaching lectures. I was growing in a way that I hadn't experienced since my early twenties. These were exciting times for everyone as we were growing so much in numbers that they began to talk about building. At that time they were renting a space under a grocery store and had to set up and tear down all the equipment each week to accommodate the needs of others who used that space on weekdays. That's such a pain, but Chris and the leadership team faithfully did it over and over for years before finally obtaining a building of their own.

A New Chapter

The Elders wanted to form a special task team to look into alternative services, and Mark asked Laura and me to join this very elite group. There were more master's degrees in that room than Harvard could boast and we were pretty intimidated by their combined level of experience and education. The remarkable thing about this group of highly accomplished men and women was that they were so determined to keep their hands off and not steer the ship in any personal direction that nothing was ever really done toward the original purpose in coming together. In fact, when the subject of alternative services even came up, it was quickly thrust back down lest we take hold of it instead of the Holy Spirit. Even though we never explored that subject at length, it was still a wonderful time of fellowship for the year that we were together and I learned a lot from these godly people. Neither Laura nor I had ever been part of a Bible study before (yes, you read it right). We sort of morphed into a small group instead of a task force and were now supposed to be doing life together — and it was even expressed that we should be each other's best friends. I don't believe that happens upon request. I also quickly formed the opinion that "real life" doesn't happen in a circle; good conversations can happen, but there's something artificial about sitting and facing each other that instantly kills what you're trying to achieve. A circle is antimatter to life's matter. Think about sharing your deepest pain and secrets with a friend; would you feel more relaxed and comfortable while having coffee, or on your back on a couch? I recognized that the true state of our doing life together happened upon arrival and existed in its purest form for the first fifteen minutes as we visited, and then ended as soon as the bell was struck and it was time to begin. "Ding! Ding! Ding!" Unnatural silence and expectation took over.

You might ask what right a complete novice should have to an opinion at all. I guess the advantage to being green was that our lack of experience allowed us to be completely malleable and see it from a fresh and virginal perspective. I still have a lot of respect for the people in that group, but I discovered a curious thing about growth and maturity that I wasn't aware of before. At a certain point, you can start becoming a little agitated inside and discontented with how others are doing something and start thinking along the lines of, "If this was my group, I'd...." It may sound like someone being critical, and it could take that unfortunate avenue, but hopefully it's a sign of something much healthier and productive. It could be a restlessness that comes from reaching a point when you're ready to take the reins yourself. It's not that someone is even necessarily doing it wrong, but maybe your own unique vision is starting to rise to the top and you find yourself desiring to express and bring about its fruition.

The worst thing you can do is to reach over the driver's shoulder from the backseat and try to commandeer the steering wheel. This is their car! Let them go in the direction they felt led to travel. Maybe it's time to buy your own car and drive. The seeds were now planted in me for a later purpose that I wouldn't be aware of for some time yet.

We eventually decided to disband after a year of being together and Laura and I found another group that sounded interesting. It was mainly composed of mountain climbers and was very different from the group we had been with. From seasoned professionals to street-smart intelligentsia — what a ride! Absolutely anything went with this collection of individuals; there was no limit to the range of topics we could and would bring up, and since someone different led each week, everyone had a chance to be heard. That arrangement could bring about directionless chaos with the wrong people, but it didn't here. These hearts were devoted followers of Christ and still childlike enough in their inquiry to provide stimulating conversations and debates. And yet, over time, I began to feel those same subtle frustrations with some of our methods. I was learning what I liked and didn't like and that would serve a purpose, too. Our Rocky Mountain pastor, Jess, and his sweet wife, Deb, came to visit this group and really liked it and wanted to join. Unfortunately, the founders felt like we were already at the max so Jess and Deb were kindly informed that they couldn't be a part of our group. I totally understood and yet I was disappointed because I liked this couple a lot.

You Want to Do What?!

Now, the unthinkable happened (drums please). I found myself contemplating starting our own small group so we could include Jess and Deb. This was serious anarchy. "Who's running this ship?!" I might have asked myself. "Are you going to let some mutinous, scurvy pirate take the ship and steer us over the edge into oblivion, Cap'n?" Okay, a little dramatic perhaps, but only a little. You can't truly know what an alien and revolutionary thought this was after nurturing my rebellion for ten years (actually, as far back as I can remember). When you start having internal conversations of this nature, it might not be a bad idea to have some coffee with a friend *and* lie on the couch for a while! I couldn't believe this was me thinking about leading a Bible study. Is that what it was going to be — a Bible study? There were already millions of those around. The teeter-totter began to shift in the other direction as I thought about a bunch of Ned Flanders in a room together. Man, you had better think about this carefully...

The vital difference this time was that I had been totally transformed on the inside and could now see a brand-new vista of possibilities, similar to when I had suddenly realized that I could move my woodworking equipment around to suit my individual needs as a cabinet maker so many years ago at the Y. Was it possible to provide something unique that would fill in the gaps as I saw them? I thought back over the last two years and what I had learned from my many wise friends in those groups, and what I could add to that. I had lots of ideas and was getting excited, but there was still a squatter named Resistance, occupying my resident thoughts that I could be a leader in this area. There's another element that finally tipped the scales that

I long to tell you about, but I don't feel free to do that. It's something between the Lord and me that seems too private to divulge openly. Suffice it to say that there was a strong dialog taking place between me and my Savior for several weeks before I finally became convinced that it was His will for me to go forward.

It seems absurd and more than a little blasphemous for me to say that I agreed to...but with conditions. And yet, that's exactly what took place. I said in effect, "Okay, I'll do it, but this is the way I'm coming in...." Please hear me: as soon as I said it, I felt Him smile. It was as if my rebellions were His all along and He was simply waiting for me to realize I had an ally. I wasn't sure how Laura would feel about being involved in yet another group so I was a little hesitant to ask her — but she was the one who brought it up first! That was an incredible confirmation because she didn't feel very comfortable in a group larger than four, or six at most. Her desire to try it within our own layout and design was extremely encouraging and I was amazed at her courage and fortitude. I e-mailed Jess and Deb and proposed the idea. They both liked the initial idea and we made a date for them to come over and talk about the details. Nothing is better than chocolate fondue to fill the room with hope and an optimistic atmosphere, not to mention an excuse for indulging in a forbidden treat! These were some of our ideas and foundational mandates as we presented them to Jess and Deb:

- We didn't want to be just another sign-up group doing traditional Bible study.
- We wanted to hand-choose those who we knew were struggling with God or church. (Outsiders like

ourselves, in other words.)

- Doing Life Together means actually doing the things we do in life — together! Hiking, watching movies, camping, etc. All of that was just as important as studying and praying together. Friendship and trust has to build naturally, or not at all.

- It had to be absolutely safe to share our deepest pain and dramas with each other.

- No question was out of bounds. You could share your most silly or complex questions about scripture — doubt of God's goodness, sex in heaven — anything at all without fear of being looked down on. We would walk together down any road or subject.

This beautiful couple responded with complete grace and affirmation. I would like to think that our providing Krispy Kreme donut holes dipped in chocolate didn't have anything to do with it! Jess had to be careful in what he endorsed because Rocky Mountain was on the verge of launching a Home Church initiative and there were certain guidelines he would need to abide by. To be honest, I was never that comfortable with being called a church, except in the sense that any amount of believers gathered together is a church in the Lord's eyes. To me, we were simply a bunch of friends getting together and loving each other and the Lord, and we didn't need a title or description. I wanted it to be real and natural. All my "rebellions" only related to things that fell outside of those simple parameters. That's why I felt Him smile. Seems He wants the same thing, too.

Our first dinner together at Jess and Deb's was filled with twelve precious souls, and it was amazing to witness what happens when the Lord is leading something. Most of us didn't know each other, but everyone seemed to relax immediately and an unaccountable trust formed. I felt I had to lead by example, so I started off by describing our purpose in starting this group and shared some of my own struggles. The amazing thing was that almost everyone present opened up some of the darkest experiences in their lives among people they had never met; in some cases, they shared things they had never shared with anyone else before. You can't force or manufacture that kind of atmosphere on your own. It had to be His Spirit blessing our new endeavor. The same thing happened the following week. We were bonding as a family quickly and I was thrilled to be a small part of this. As I watched Him at work, I realized how little I had to do with what was unfolding before my eyes. This was unprecedented in so many of our experiences and we all embraced the rare opportunity to find comfort, strength and safety in each other's company. A beautiful thing, indeed.

Chapter 28

A Rocky Start

I was new to this leader business and I certainly made my mistakes, but I was also growing so much and discovering things about myself that I didn't know before. I wanted us to have a variety of experiences, so we would study books, watch videos, read scripture, pray together, have pizza parties, and sometimes just visit. Something I learned during a longer video series called the *Truth Project* was that we couldn't go very long without personal sharing time because our intimacy as a group suffered. This was a very good indication of how much we needed each other now and we changed our schedule to include having an evening to talk and catch up every third week. As I got to know each individual better, I started recognizing their areas of strength and tried to nurture them as much as possible. I also wanted everyone to feel free to explore areas that they weren't so confident in, like leading one of our meetings or praying out loud for example — any area in which they wanted to grow. It wasn't a matter of doing something well, it was about practicing in front of friends that supported you and wouldn't laugh when (not if) you screwed up. If we truly had a safe environment, why not use it?

Deb's mother, Betty, introduced us to a place that she volunteered in once a month down in Loveland called The Community Kitchen. We signed up as a group to volunteer once a month with her and had a wonderful time serving the homeless together. This kind of environment revealed where each person's comfort level was. Some liked to be out front visiting with the people; some liked to fill their plates with food and have some contact; others wanted to be back in the kitchen, cooking and washing up with minimal contact. It was all good and practically illustrated Christ's description of us as different parts of the same body, each doing our part and yet completing a larger purpose as a whole. Everyone has a gift and unique personality and they are happiest and most fulfilled when serving within their capacity and design. We would often go to Sonic Burger afterward and relive our time together at the Kitchen. Some patrons were very fun and sweet, some could be prickly and one or two bordered on hostility if you said the wrong thing. One in particular would become very aggressive if you asked him more than two successive questions:

1) "How are you?
2) "Do you want potatoes?"
Stop!

Learning to Lead

As of this writing, our group has now been together for over seven years. We go camping each summer, visit Water World, maybe take in a Rockies game. Having fun together is such an important element and balances our study time. Each group is different and you have to discern the alchemy you have and ask for the wisdom in how to best nurture and facilitate it. We had some leave for one reason or another and others would come in. Presently we have fifteen in our family and that is pretty large for our purpose, but it's rare to have all of us together at the same time anyway, so we usually do just fine as we take turns hosting.

Another adjustment I had to make was the recognition that you can't make everyone happy all the time. After a couple of years of just being happy to be together, it's natural for people to start pointing out what they like and don't like. Some want to study scripture only. Some don't want to study at all and want to party all the time, party all the time, party all the time! The best I can do is to provide a variety of opportunities and then it's up to everyone else to exhibit graciousness when we're doing something they don't enjoy as much. Absolutely no problem for this family. Graciousness pours out of them effortlessly. Speaking of grace, I have to give kudos to pastor Jess Mahon for his amazing patience and self-control in letting me lead our family in ways that had to push him to the limit sometimes, especially considering his thirty-plus years of ministry experience. Thank you, Sir, for always being there anytime I needed advice, but never trying to exert control when my newly developing style strayed off your firm theological path. I do have to confess to the pleasure I feel in being a friendly thorn in your side — especially regarding science.

Coming into Rocky Mountain, I know that I was carrying a small chip on my shoulder regarding my interest and taste in secular art, music, and literature. Part of my rebellion and condition in returning to church was that I refused to be ashamed of what I read or listened to. I knew His Spirit was in me and if I had permission and freedom to do something, I wouldn't allow another human being to persuade me otherwise. Neither did I have any intention in promoting this attitude or causing someone else to stumble, but I wouldn't hide it, either. A very funny occasion happened when my sister came running up to me one Saturday night. She was so excited because she met a woman who loved Rush as much as I did. I could hardly believe it, but I allowed Lee Ann to tow me across the room to meet her. What I saw made it even harder to believe because she just didn't look the part. Hard to imagine her playing air guitar or drums, which no true fan can resist doing when one of Rush's songs comes on. Lee Ann introduced me and I said how cool it was that she liked them, too.

"Oh yeah!" she said. "I listen every time he's on the radio."
Hmm… "He," as in Mr. Jethro Tull? or Sir Led Zeppelin? or "By the way, which one's Pink (Floyd)?"
"What's a favorite of yours?" I asked with growing suspicion.
"Everything," she replied. This was just too much and I suddenly had a BFO (Blinding Flash of the Obvious):
"You're talking about Rush Limbaugh, aren't you?"
Bingo.

HP

At that time (2003), Harry Potter mania was strong and a growing concern in many churches. Was J. K. Rowling promoting witchcraft? I wasn't interested in the series at all, not because of fear, but because I suspected anything the mass public embraced so completely. I kept resisting my sister's persistent urgings to read one of the books, but finally caved after she bought me a hardcover copy of *Harry Potter and the*

Sorcerer's Stone for my birthday. I now felt I had to at least try it out of respect for her thoughtful purchase. I was hooked after three pages. I now understood why Rowling was richer than the Queen of England. She was a marvelous writer, so funny and creative in character development! Laura was reading a paperback version at the same time and was equally taken by the story line and Rowling's intelligent humor. We both devoured the whole series as far as she had written it to that point. When the final book was released, we bought two copies to take with us to Maine so we could read them at the same time. We had rented a small home in Bethany for a week, one that was literally right on the lake's edge. It had a covered porch running all the way around the house and we sat out there reading the books in their entirety while the eye of a downgraded hurricane tracked precisely up our street, bringing torrential rain for a couple of days. Quite a rare memory.

This series wasn't promoting witchcraft: it was good vs. evil just like *The Chronicles of Narnia* or *The Lord of the Rings*, with good being the obvious favorite. If I saw any danger at all, it was because her writing was so good and appealing that it might make the unprotected young reader curious enough to research their way into real danger, via magick and the occult. A good friend's son was very interested in reading the series and he was concerned about the content being a bad influence. I asked him if he had read it. He said no, and I suggested that maybe he should so he would know firsthand instead of going by someone else's opinion. Or he and his son could read it together and it would be an opportunity to talk about it, whether good or bad. That's probably what my mother would have thought of and done.

Untainted Reward

I made a very good friend on our worship team named Steve Tindle who had almost identical taste in music, even the obscure stuff that almost no one else had heard of. Unfortunately, because of his past indulgences before becoming a believer, he didn't feel the freedom to go back and listen to those old bands. Because I had never done any drugs and there was only clean and healthy association with that music, so I could — and still do find myself going back and enjoying everything from my youth. I know this will be hard for some people in the church community to understand, but a lot of this music can lift my heart up in praise to God because of the sheer brilliance and creativity inherent in it. I'm talking about the music itself and not necessarily the lyrics, although they were often just as creative, no matter what the topic was about. The reason why it affected me that way is this: God gave everyone their talent and abilities and when they do such marvelous works, my heart naturally praises God for it, regardless of whether they acknowledge that it came from God or not. I know where it came from. The same is true for art, literature, or making movies. Talent is talent, no matter where it's found, just as truth is truth, independent of where you find it. Wisdom is found all over the earth and in every religion — therefore I can potentially learn from any one of them without necessarily adopting the parent belief. I am not accountable for what they do with it or to whom they give credit, and this acknowledgment gives me the freedom to explore and enjoy the world instead of just limiting my experience and appreciation to only that which has the approved label "Christian" on it. It's not necessary to know the personal beliefs of Roger Federer in order to appreciate the fluid elegance and almost ballet-like grace of his tennis playing style. He is simply the best male player in history and we count it a great privilege to have seen him play live.

Music in particular is so wonderful because of its neutrality. It evokes emotions that range anywhere from tenderness to joy, heartbreak to hope, or from adrenaline to anger. It's analog and continuous in that there are no intermediate steps within one emotion, or even between different kinds. A piano and guitar have increments of pitch, a violin has none. A single song can take you through the whole spectrum effortlessly. I wonder sometimes if there is a physiological cause; that our bodies physically vibrate in pleasing ways to certain waveforms and musical intervals before being converted to electrical impulses for our brain to interpret. That would help explain why everyone's taste in music is so subjective. I suspect that the same is true about food; that each person tastes it slightly differently. As I say, if you tasted cheese the way I taste cheese, you wouldn't eat it either. I don't believe music has a spiritual side to it, I believe music is spiritual and has a physical side to it. In the same way that mathematician Alan Turing found a way to bridge pure logic with practical reality via mechanical processes, maybe music is the bridge between Heaven and our physical universe. It certainly melts the ice off my wings when nothing else can reach me.

Preprogrammed for Pleasure

This brings me to another thought: how does our brain know how to interpret taste, sound, waveforms, sight, and scent? I understand that hearing is mechanical and smell is chemical, but eventually all our senses become electrical as they enter neuronal passages. And no matter how exquisitely intricate the human eye is, the brain has to already know how to form the images. Just like a Cray supercomputer, it doesn't matter how sophisticated the circuitry is, somebody has to write the software and instructions for it to know what to do. Especially in the case of scent, I'm not satisfied with the explanation that it was stored up and passed down through evolution. At whatever hypothetical stage of primitive development you choose, the brain of antiquity still had to make sense of it to evoke the sensation of smell as we recognize it now. It's unfair to point out a specific chemical reaction as proof that it simply happened because of its inherent nature, because you're "joining regularly scheduled programming already in progress." Nothing in the physical universe can be inherent because when you trace it back far enough, it's simply one primitive and identical atom interacting with another. Even the idea of heavier elements in the periodic table being created within the interior nuclear furnace of massive stars is making an inexplicable assumption that it happened because it had to, but I see that as a cop-out. Whatever pure energy formed our physical universe, it had to be ruled by pre-existing purpose and explicit directions on how to behave. Again, you can't start with a program already in progress in explaining the behavior of the most elementary particles, whether they be quarks or yet smaller strings of energy. They received information from somewhere. If anything has an inherent nature, it's because someone made them that way. The Bible proclaims that God made all things through Jesus, and in two thousand years of constant challenge and endless bombardment, no one has ever been able to discredit what scripture proclaims as true: that there was a man named Jesus and that He rose from the grave. In fact, it's just the opposite. Historical and archaeological evidence always supports what the Bible said was true all along. No one has ever provided a truly reasonable alternative as to how and why we exist in my opinion, and so I believe — and love Him — for to merely believe is not enough.

I never really thought about it before writing this book, but I am coming to the opinion that every possible scent we could ever encounter already existed in our brains in the form of digital software. From the first moment that we breathe air, it's simply a matter of matching up the air molecules with the preset we were already given. I love to talk about this kind of thing with believer and nonbeliever alike. It's fascinating to explore His handiwork in both the macro and the micro.

Chapter 29

For Every Step

For every step we take away from God, life becomes more complicated. It's a very simple truth.

One rule in the Garden of Eden becomes ten commandments, which then becomes six hundred thirteen rabbinical laws. Today, we have endless national ideologies and constitutions attempting to explain and govern our individual behavior. Where does it end? Science reveals His design and exploits it for our good (mostly), but then we turn around and use it as evidence against His existence. We travel to other planets with the hope that one day we will be able to carry humanity to other worlds for a more utopian existence. The only problem is that wherever we go, there we are. The major problem is inside us, not outside. Why is it that when someone becomes unhinged mentally, they never let loose in a frenzy of mowing people's yards and bringing groceries to the elderly in unbridled excess? When the gate of self-control unexpectedly flies open, where does the ravenous desire to hurt and destroy come from? Why doesn't the murderous lunatic ever run into a mall and shout out, "The reincarnated Buddha told me to shoot everyone!" Sounds like a devilish plot of accusation against God, to me. Everything that exists out there in the way of rules and guidelines is to help us control and suppress our natural state as it has existed since the Fall. This says a lot about the supposedly pure and holy "Self" that only awaits our "actualization," doesn't it? Yes, we can and should improve our world and try to remove the oppression and cruelty that dominates so much of our planet, even today. But no environmental condition, no matter how perfect, will address the restlessness and desire for true purpose built within each of our hearts. And even if we do live a long and wonderful life, we still die — and then what?

Remember that I love science, and it makes no difference to my faith whether the universe is six thousand or fourteen billion years old; I still maintain that God made it. For all the good science does, it wrongly spills over into our philosophical world, trying to explain the "why" instead of the more objective and profitable "what" and "how." Pure science left us long ago and most scientists now operate with their own ideology that is every bit as stringent and exclusive as any religion you can find. I can understand their perspective in part because for thousands of years, we attributed everything in nature that we couldn't understand to be the mysteries of God, simply because we didn't have the knowledge to understand how things work. The problem now is that by discovering and explaining the physical processes by which He designed and accomplishes His purpose in the physical world, scientists think that there is now no need for Him to exist. This is just as ridiculous and absurd as if your child, having been given a set of Lincoln Logs by you, might build something impressive and determine by doing so that you didn't exist. In my opinion, it's not a matter of there being an intellectual barrier to believing in God, it's a matter of control. People don't want God to exist because it would then require accountability, and they wouldn't be able to live their lives however they please. Moreover, there's the personal affront of admitting there's something they can never explain. That's unacceptable to many.

Life Becomes More Complicated

There's a wonderful Bugs Bunny cartoon we grew up with that demonstrates this perfectly. Little Red Riding Hood meets the wolf in the woods and asks directions to her grandmother's house. He points down a road that you can see winding its way up and down hills, finally disappearing and reappearing over the horizon. She thanks him and begins singing as she heads off into the distance. The "camera" pans a little to the right, and there's her grandmother's house, twenty feet away.

She was so close to her destination, but instead, she ends up traveling untold distances and enduring who knows what to just end up almost where she began. Such is our journey when we walk away from our only source of fulfillment and joy, seeking illusions of grandeur and trying to fill the resulting vacuum with endless "things" that are, in reality, nothing more than cotton candy — momentarily sweet, but without any life-giving nutrition whatsoever. I would love to say that once I found a true relationship with my Creator, I stayed close to home and didn't — as Gollum warned — follow the "tricksy lights." Unfortunately, I did — and still often do. Wait, there's one now…

One thing I have noticed in the last few years is that my protective leash is shorter than it once was. He doesn't allow me to wander as far before I feel the tug, drawing me back to safety. The things of this world are truly growing strangely dim as I set my eyes and hope on that Greater Morning. I'm finally growing a little deaf to the siren's call. I at least now know where my true joy doesn't lie.

Yes, even after fifty-four years on this earth, there are many things I don't understand about God, Jesus, and Heaven, but I know enough to believe and place my trust there. Really, what do I have to lose? I go through this life with hope and if I'm totally wrong, there won't be anyone on the other side to say, "I told you so!" But what are the alternative consequences? My mother used to wisely say, "I'd rather believe and be wrong than not believe and be wrong." I have no idea what's ahead of me in this life or when I'll be called Home, but I want my remaining time and effort to be eternal in nature. Success and riches mean something completely different now and I don't want (or need) to waste my time with unnecessary pursuits. As far as sharing my faith with others, I don't want to "tell" people about Jesus, because almost everyone has heard about Him already. I do want to help unravel the religious distortions that prevent people I care about from knowing and understanding the truth of who He really is and how profoundly they are loved and adored. I want them to know and believe there is hope that can't be shaken or taken away from those who believe and trust in Christ. I don't want to tell people what to believe, but I do want to walk side-by-side together and remove false barriers and help enable them to reason well and make their own decision based on fact and truth instead.

Let's Make a Deal

If you inherited a storage unit from a distant relative whom you hardly knew, and some stranger approached you and offered a certain amount for its contents, would you take it? Who of us would be gullible enough not to at least go through everything first to see what you had before taking money for it? You might be giving up diamonds or gold bars or an undiscovered Renoir for next to nothing in return. And yet that's exactly what we all do every day. God tells us everything here is temporary and not to accumulate wealth on earth because we will only lose it when we die — that only our decisions, love for each other, and service done in His name will survive with us into the next life. Do you remember the game show *Let's Make a Deal* from the '60s and '70s? Contestants were often given the offer of $50 or $100 in cash right then, or they could take a chance and see what the mystery gift was. It could be a box of crackers or it might be a brand-new sports car — you never knew! There are rewards promised to His children that we have no idea of their value, and yet we find ourselves trading them for a sinful indulgence here and there because it's immediate and pleasurable. We have absolutely no idea what we are giving up in exchange. Think about a toy you just *had* to have when you were a child. Looking back at it now, is it still so wonderful and fulfilling that you would be willing to forego every adult gift and privilege you have enjoyed since? What is a Big Wheel compared to learning to drive and buying a Porsche, or flying a jet? We are playing with childrens's toys here, and nothing this world has to offer is worth missing Heaven over. Even a kind word or cup of water offered to a stranger could end up with a worth far exceeding our most coveted treasure here. That being said, I believe it's for our own good that we're not told anything more about those rewards, because we could easily take our eyes off the Lord and focus on the treasure instead ("Gimme! Gimme! Gimme!"). Heaven will be beyond anything we can imagine; not because of rewards, but because our endless cravings and misplaced desires will finally be fulfilled as we look into the eyes of our Creator for the very first time — and truly understand our worth and purpose in existing. Life doesn't end here, nor do our personalities and the things we enjoy; but we will seamlessly continue without frustration or resistance as our God-given abilities and gifts unfold throughout eternity in the undiminished love and care of our Father.

One Street Off Main

For all my trials and tribulations, I have had a blessed life and often lay my head on my pillow at night with thanksgiving in my heart and on my lips as I whisper a final prayer. Whatever the current burden is in your own life, please know that something far greater is awaiting those who place their childlike trust in the only Savior that we need, Jesus. It's okay to have unanswered questions and points of rebellion (as I still do) and still be a follower of Christ. It's okay, and preferable in my opinion, to look, sound, and think differently than the masses you encounter in church and in life. He made each of us to be unique and to reflect a different aspect of Him, and our world is much, much better and more colorful when we stay true to how we were made. Being conformed to the image of Christ doesn't narrow us down as it might sound; it paradoxically frees us from all the fears and prejudices that weigh us down and allows each of us to truly be what we were meant to be. It also enables us to love others unconditionally because our own insatiable need for acceptance and security is already met.

I really do see myself as being one street off Main, but that's okay because it's less noisy and the scenery is far sweeter over here. Understanding what truly makes me happy as an individual, and yielding my often misplaced ambitions to God's greater truth and wisdom concerning eternity, frees me to live each day without the need to compete and compare myself to others around me. The freedom and liberty this affords me can't be adequately captured by words alone — it will probably require me to write new music!

To download my albums or buy CDs,
go to iTunes or CD Baby

Acknowledgements

Editing and Proofing:
Kathleen Puahau Aki
Contact: puahau.aki@gmail.com

Cover Design:
Laura Geppinger

Consulting:
Jason Kelly
Anna Oberg
Niki Barlow
Laura Edwards
Dan Decker

Bibliography

C. S. Lewis, *The Weight of Glory,* |New York York: MacMillan Company, 1949|

J. K. Rowling, *Harry Potter and the Chamber of Secrets,* [New York City: Sholastic, 1998]

C. S. Lewis, *Surprised By Joy,* [San Diego: Harcourt, 1955]

42602552R00151

Made in the USA
Charleston, SC
02 June 2015